# Connecting to Kink

A collection of essays, tips, personal experience, and opinion written from more than a dozen years of experience advising online kinksters. Whether you just discovered online kink, tried unsuccessfully to connect with someone, or want to satisfy your curiosity, you will find useful information about how safely exploring your BDSM fantasies online.

"I.G. Frederick does what few other BDSM writers and practitioners have done, acknowledging that many find their way into kink online. This book offers vital guidance on how to sensibly and safely explore the issues and the landscape - virtually first, and then in the flesh."

Remittance Girl, author of
*Gaijin* and *The Waiting Room*

# Acknowledgments

This book would not have reached your hands without the help of many friends and colleagues. I thank my readers and supporters, especially Laurie, my dear friend and editor; Shawn, first reader; and of course, Patrick, my boy, my love, my muse, my webmaster. Thanks also to all those I have corresponded with online and off and those who have served me, well and ill, over the years. I have learned something from each one of you and I hope that you find what you seek. Thanks also to Chris, aka TheDarkLord, whose request for the presentation that became Chapter 11 was the inspiration for this book.

# Connecting to Kink

## Safely exploring your BDSM fantasies online

# I.G. Frederick
### NLA:I Award Winning Author

*Connecting to Kink*
© **2015 by I.G. Frederick**

ISBN: 978-1-937471-39-2

**Pussy Cat Press**
**http://pussycatpress.com/publisher.html/**
**P.O. Box 19764**
**Portland OR 97280**

Original illustrations on pages viii, 4, and 24 Copyright © 2015 by Pussy Cat Press
Top photograph on page 50 Copyright © 2015 by Pussy Cat Press
Author photo on page vii by Nyla Alisia
Book covers on page 36 from Laura Antoniou's *Marketplace* series http://lantoniou.com/ and Cecilia Tan's *Struck by Lightning* series blog.ceciliatan.com/
Screen capture page 70 from a portion of list on http://oopomo.com/checklist.html
Photo on page 104 © by David Shankbone http://commons.wikimedia.org/wiki/User:David_Shankbone
Flogger and photos on pages 12, 30, 42, 60, 64, 70, 90, 96, 100, and bottom photo on page 50 © Depositphotos.com

All rights reserved. No part of this work may be reproduced or utilized in any form or by any means, electronic or mechanical, or by any information storage and retrieval system, without permission in writing from the author, except by reviewers who may quote brief excerpts in connection with a review.

Readers should be aware that the activities and behaviors discussed in this book carry an inherent risk of emotional, mental, financial, and/or physical harm. Anyone who participates in the type of activities described in this book must personally accept the risk of doing so. By reading this book, you agree to accept the information as the opinion of the author and you agree to accept that the author and publisher assume no responsibility for any damage experienced by or caused by any person who reads all or part of this book.

# Table of Contents

Acknowledgments ..................................................................... ii
About the Author ..................................................................... vii
Introduction ............................................................................. 1
Chapter One ............................................................................. 5
   *Writing a Profile* ................................................................ *5*
Chapter Two ............................................................................ 13
   *Terminology & Acronyms* ................................................ *13*
Chapter Three ......................................................................... 25
   *Labels* .................................................................................. *25*
Chapter Four .......................................................................... 31
   *Dynamics* ........................................................................... *31*
Chapter Five ........................................................................... 37
   *Fantasy vs Reality* ............................................................. *37*
Chapter Six ............................................................................. 43
   *BDSM vs abuse* ................................................................. *43*
Chapter Seven ........................................................................ 51
   *Staying Safe Online* ........................................................... *51*
Chapter Eight ......................................................................... 61
   *The Numbers* .................................................................... *61*
Chapter Nine .......................................................................... 65
   *Staying Safe if You Venture Out* ...................................... *65*
Chapter Ten ............................................................................ 71
   *Understanding Erotic Power Exchange* ......................... *71*

Chapter Eleven ........................................................................ 79
   *Confirming Consent* ............................................................ 79
Chapter Twelve ....................................................................... 91
   *Courting a FemDom* ............................................................ 91
Chapter Thirteen .................................................................... 97
   *A Word On ProDommes (aka Dominatrixes)* ....................... 97
Chapter Fourteen ................................................................. 101
   *Munches* ........................................................................... 101
Chapter Fifteen .................................................................... 105
   *What About Dungeons?* ..................................................... 105
Chapter Sixteen ................................................................... 109
   *Resources* ......................................................................... 109

# About the Author

I.G. Frederick trades words for cash, specializing in erotic and transgressive fiction and poetry since 2001. Her short stories appear in *Hustler Fantasies*, *Forum*, *Foreplay*, and *Desire Presents*, as well as in electronic, audio, and print anthologies. Her fiction and poetry celebrate finding love in BDSM relationships from the authority of one enjoying that for more than a decade.

A former newspaper reporter and trained observer, I.G. Frederick also watches the many ways human interactions turn ugly. She writes about abusive and tragic relationships as Korin I. Dushayl.

In addition, I.G. Frederick shares her BDSM knowledge and experience in her nonfiction work. She won the National Leather Association — International Cynthia Slater Nonfiction Article Award in 2014, received the Rose & Thorn Leather Woman of the Year award in 2008, and presents on various topics at area events.

A FemDom, Ms. Frederick owns the man she adores. Although dominant in the rest of his life, he demonstrates his love by serving as her submissive.

You can learn more and find free samples of her writing on her websites:

*http://eroticawriter.net and*
*http://transgressivewriter.com*

only online

only in the
bedroom

once in
a while

only at
parties

S&M
only

D/s
only

24/7

# Introduction

Like gender and sexuality, BDSM has always existed on a fluid continuum. The ubiquitousness of the Internet has had three significant impacts on that spectrum. The first is that it's become much easier, because of the information available online, for people to figure out where they fit on the spectrum. Second, because more people have found ways to connect to kink communities via the Internet, specialized communities have developed that serve specific segments of the spectrum rather than everyone involved in any type of kink. And third, the continuum has expanded to include people who only get involved with kink online.

Many practitioners of BDSM in real life denigrate those who only participate online. But, under the concept of *Your Kink Is Not My Kink but that's okay* (YKINMK) I've come to believe we should accept online players as what they are — another type of kink.

I spent many years online when I was single. I still maintain profiles on some sites to promote my writing. As a result of my online activities, I met people who have become dear friends. I found men who served me for a few weeks to a few months to more than a year, some of whom are still a part of my life. I met folks I enjoyed whipping and beating. I invited online kinksters to participate in the local munch, some of whom are running it now. And, one troubled young man I corresponded with at length, with whom I spoke for hours on the telephone but who I never met, became the inspiration for two of my books.

There is a tremendous difference between online and real-life kink. Although some make the transition from online to real life, many more have no interest in doing so. To them, I offer this collection of essays, tips, personal experience, and opinion. I include advice on how to find what you want from an online partner and how to navigate the online world safely.

But, even if that's the extent of your kink and you never plan to venture into real life, limits are fluid. If you ever decide at some point that you'd like to move beyond the computer, this book also provides some tips on how to get started and safely meet up with folks in real life.

The first thing you need to understand is that one of the things that keeps many people from exploring kink in real life is embarrassment. Unfortunately, our society has a lot of hang-ups when it comes to sex. For decades, homosexuality was classified as a mental disease. Until very recently, sadism, masochism, and a host of other paraphilias and sexual fetishes were considered mental illnesses. Now they're only listed as "paraphilic disorders" if an individual's fetishes cause them distress, impairment, personal harm, or risk of harm to others.

Of course that creates a Catch 22. Because BDSM is stigmatized and misunderstood, someone who pursues an interest in BDSM could experience that stigmatization and misunderstanding. The stigmatization and misunderstanding they experience is likely to cause distress. That distress might be diagnosed by a professional to be within the parameters of a "paraphilic disorder." Yet, in reality it's the stigmatization and misunderstanding from others, rather than any paraphilia itself, that causes the distress.

The Internet has helped many people discover that, however bizarre they believe their particular fetish is, they can find a whole group of people who enjoy the same fetish. And no matter how disgusting they might believe their fetish is, they can probably find people who have a fetish that they consider even more obnoxious.

Whether you're just discovering online kink, have been trying unsuccessfully to make a connection, or are just curious, you will find something useful in these pages. Just remember never jump into anything before you're ready. Be safe, and have fun learning more about yourself, other people, and the many choices available to you.

- pansexual/omnisexual
- bisexual
- heteroflexible/homoflexible
- monosexual (straight/homosexual)
- asexual

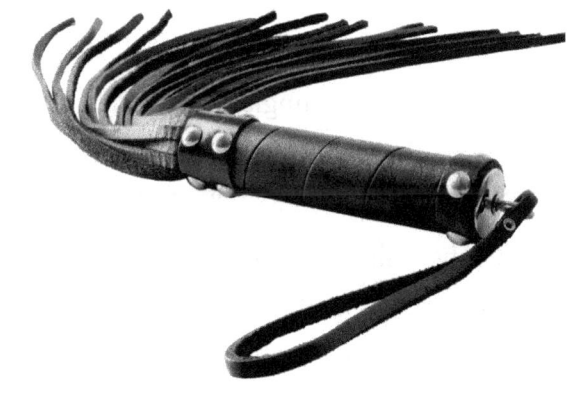

# Chapter One
## Writing a Profile

According to the *American Heritage Dictionary,* a profile is "A biographical essay presenting the subject's most noteworthy characteristics and achievements."

## "I Don't Know What to Say Here"

I could take a round-the-world cruise — possibly two — if I had a dollar for every online profile I've read that started with (or consisted solely of) some form of "I don't know what to say here." That tidbit will get you absolutely *no* response, unless you're female and post hot photographs of yourself. (See Chapter 8.) When I see this phrase, I wonder if they really can't figure out what to write or if they're just too lazy to put forth the effort.

For those who fall in the former category, the trick to online success is to be specific. Meaningless platitudes and clichés will only work against you. Too many "profiles" contain little more than vague generalities: "seeking owner," "looking to serve," "looking for training," "seeking a slave," "looking for a unicorn."

Instead of dashing off something generic, take the time to think about how you want to present yourself: Why might someone find you of interest? What do you have to offer? Why have you come to this particular site? What do you hope to find?

Buzzwords are more off-putting than noteworthy. Do better than writing "extremely submissive and masochistic" or "well trained, obedient, and totally submissive" or "natural Dominant." Distinctive details will help you stand out from the crowd, especially if you're male.

(More on this in Chapter 8.)

You're more likely to get noticed if your profile begins with what you have to offer and then discusses what you seek. The more articulate and precise you are, the more likely you will get responses that could lead to the type of interaction you want.

*If* you haven't decided what you're looking for yet, just be honest. You can put "lurking" and folks will ignore you until you figure things out and write something more appropriate. Better to just watch and read at first. If you interact with someone and alienate them, they'll block you and you'll never be able to contact them again unless you start over with a new profile.

Be yourself. Don't try too hard to be funny. If humor comes naturally, by all means play it up. But, don't force it.

If you use the journal function many sites offer, the same rules apply — present yourself as you want to be perceived. For example, don't whine unless you want to be perceived as a whiner.

## Vocabulary

Learn the difference between Dominant and dominate, something many online seem to have difficulty with. Dominant is used both as a noun and an adjective. Dominate is a verb. If you put in your profile that you're seeking a dominate or that you want to dominant someone, many will consider you illiterate and refuse to communicate — unless they also don't know the difference. (See more about BDSM labels in Chapter 3.)

## Honesty & Consistency

Make sure any photograph you post is consistent with your profile. If you hold yourself out as a sissy maid, but photograph yourself all dolled up in your crisp black uniform standing in a horribly sloppy setting that looks like it hasn't been cleaned in weeks, you've just destroyed any credibility you might have gained from the uniform. If you claim to be a FemDom but post a photograph of yourself posing nude with a collar around your neck, you're contradicting yourself. (See more about photographs in Chapter 7.)

Don't identify as a submissive if you're actually a bottom looking to fulfill your sexual fantasies. (Unfortunately many sites do not give you the option of choosing "bottom" instead of "submissive," so be clear about what you seek in your profile.) If you try to convince Dominants that you're a submissive by using words like "well trained" and "obedient," but then go on to discuss how much you enjoy pain, bondage, and punishment, that inconsistency indicates you're probably not a submissive at all.

Submissive means you submit to a Dominant's desires and whims. If you wish to dictate how they dress, how they treat you, or what they will do with you, then you're not a submissive. If you're mostly seeking, pain, bondage, humiliation, or fetish wear (on you or your partner), you're probably a bottom.

Nothing wrong with being a bottom. But it's not honest to go on about how totally submissive you are when you're only interested in "submitting" during an S&M scene. Don't claim you want to serve, when you just want your ass beaten regularly. The masochist who whines that they need "discipline" multiple times a day to serve properly, probably doesn't really give a hoot about serving.

If you really just want someone to have hot kinky online sex with, don't claim you're seeking a long-term D/s real life relationship. You might get someone to correspond with you based on that assertion, but they'll dump you the minute they figure out you were dishonest.

# Create an Effective Profile

If you put some thought into the following basic questions and answer them articulately and succinctly, you will create a profile that will be stronger than many. A profile based on answers to these questions will give you a huge advantage over the "I don't know what to say" crowd. Remember to avoid personal-ad speak. Be specific, and make it positive.

- Who are you? What makes you special? You don't have to give away any personal information to answer this question. Just explain what about you would make someone else want to learn more?
- What do you bring to a potential relationship (whether online or in real life)? Don't pretend to offer more than you're willing to give.
- What type of kink are you interested in? As I said earlier, BDSM is a vast, fluid continuum. Online activities are more limited than what can be done in person, but there's still a wide variety of opportunities using words, voice, and video.
  - Do you want to be spanked for being a bad boy?
  - Do you want to pretend to be a baby girl or a puppy?
  - Are you looking for humiliation?
  - Do you enjoy requiring that someone do things to themselves or that they make you do things?
- What is your relationship status? Be honest here. If you're married and your spouse doesn't know you're looking, say so. (Yes, that will be a deal breaker for some, but it's better they know up front than find out after they've invested hours in corresponding.)
- When are you available? If you live on the west coast and only have private access to a computer between the hours of midnight and two in the morning, you won't be able to chat with someone who lives on the east coast and is in bed by nine.

# Tips

**(See Chapter 7 for tips on staying safe.)**

Sign on with a polished profile ready. Write your profile offline, *before* you ever create a profile on the site. Refine it. Check your grammar, punctuation, and spelling.

Many sites highlight new sign-ups. If you do not have your profile ready to go, you could lose the opportunity to have your full profile featured. If you start without a profile, chances are no one will check back later to see if you got around to putting one up.

Note that if you do type your profile into your browser, you can turn on the spell check function in the browser and avoid typos. (At the very least, use that function for your emails and you'll save yourself some embarrassment.)

# Correspondence

Over the years, I've had various profiles online, changing screen names and descriptions as my limits and desires evolved and my life circumstances changed. And, over the years I've received email, addressed to these different versions of myself, from some of the *same* profiles. Even if that person's screen name had changed, the email would be instantly recognizable because it was a word-for-word duplicate of what was sent previously.

You'd think if someone sent the same exact email over and over again and never received a response, they might try something different. But they don't.

*Never* use the cut and paste function. The most effective correspondence is always personal, tailored to the individual you're writing to. If you're the initiator, start by reading that person's profile. Explain how you meet the criteria they say they're looking for, and/or describe what in their profile makes you believe they meet your criteria. If they ask specific questions in their profile, answer them. And, if you're a male approaching a female, remember you're competing with dozens of others. You often can stand out just by following *her* directions about how she would like to be approached. (See Chapter 8.)

# Chapter Two
## Terminology & Acronyms

Here are some terms and acronyms you may encounter or wish to use. Many of them are discussed in more depth throughout the book. Except where noted, most terms are not gender specific. However, even gender-specific terms are not dependent on an individual's plumbing, but rather on their gender identity.

If you're new, don't be overwhelmed by all of these definitions. Just use them to help you discover what you want and need from online kink.

**24/7**
    a live-in relationship in which the power exchange never wavers

**Aftercare**
>the time spent after a BDSM scene or play session for participants to calm down, discuss events and their reactions to them, and slowly return to reality

**BBC**
>Big Black Cock

**BBW**
>Big Beautiful Woman; usually refers to someone with a belly, big breasts, and an ample ass (some consider a woman who is a size 16 and up a BBW; others insist BBW starts at size 20 or higher)

**BDSM**
>Bondage & Discipline, Dominance & Submission, Sadism & Masochism

**Bottom**
>someone who submits to bondage, training, role play, corporal punishment, but who is not necessarily emotionally committed to or in service to his/her Top/Dominant partner

**Bottom Drop**
>a temporary feeling of melancholy which a bottom can experience immediately after a BDSM scene, especially if aftercare is inadequate

**CB**
>chastity belt or device

**CBT**
>Cock and Ball Torture using clothespins, clamps, cock cages, weights, stretchers, various kinds of bindings, etc.

**CCC**
>Committed Compassionate Consensual

**Chastised**
kept in a chastity device
**Chastity Device**
a device designed to prevent a bottom/submissive from engaging in intercourse and/or masturbation
**Chastity Piercings**
piercings that can be locked together to prevent a bottom/submissive from engaging in intercourse and/or masturbation
**Collar**
(noun) a physical symbol of ownership and commitment
(verb) to take ownership
**Collared**
(adjective) owned
**Creampie Cleanup**
requiring a submissive to lick and suck ejaculate (their own or that of someone else) from a Dominant's vagina or anus
**Crossdresser**
someone who dresses in the clothing of the opposite gender (sometimes in public and attempting to pass for that gender) but who does not necessarily identify as that gender
**Cuckold/Cuckolding**
a fetish in which a bottom/submissive male accepts and/or desires that his Dominant female will entertain additional male lovers; sometimes the term is interpreted to mean that the bottom/submissive is forced to watch his Dominant have sex with another man
**D&D free**
Drug and Disease free
**D/s**
Domination and submission

**DSM**
Diagnostic & Statistical Manual of Mental Disorders

**Do Me Bottom**
a bottom who is very specific and demanding about what they want from a Top; often someone who claims to be submissive while explaining to their partner or prospective partner how to "manage" them and beat them into "submission"

**Domina/Domme**
(noun) a woman who takes control in a consensual exchange of power

**Dominant**
(noun) a person of either gender who takes control in a consensual exchange of power

(adjective) used in front of a noun to denote that the noun referred to takes control in a consensual exchange of power, e.g., a dominant woman.

**Dominate**
(verb) to take the role of Dominant in a relationship

**Domination**
an exercise of mastery or ruling power

**Dominatrix (aka ProDomme)**
a professional who tops according to the bottoms' desires/requests for specified periods of time, in exchange for financial compensation

**Dungeon**
a room or area with BDSM equipment and play space

**Erotic Power Exchange**
a consensual, temporary ceding/taking of control for an erotic encounter

**F/f**
> an interaction and/or relationship in which both the Top/Dominant and bottom/submissive are female

**F/m**
> an interaction and/or relationship in which the Top/Dominant is female and the bottom/submissive is male

**Fantasy Boy**
> a male bottom with no experience who begs a woman Top to fulfill his fantasy then runs when it's not how he imagined

**FemDom**
> a woman who takes control in a consensual exchange of power

**Fetish**
> a non-sexual object, body part, or activity that arouses a person sexually (often used to denote any erotic or sensual preference, even if it isn't part of one's sex life)

**FinDom/Financial Domme**
> a woman whose primary interaction with her customers is to take their money and/or gifts in exchange for (at most) webcam interaction

**HWP**
> Height/Weight Proportionate

**Kink**
> (noun) unconventional sexual preferences or behaviors

**Leather**
> (adjective) can refer to items made of animal hide or participants in BDSM and/or motorcycle activities (as individuals or as a community)

**Leather Family**
> a community of BDSM participants who form a unit, often with a hierarchy among members.

**Lifestyle**
used when BDSM is more than just bedroom play (this term also can apply to other sexual lifestyle choices such as swinging)

**Lifestyler**
someone who lives the lifestyle

**Limit**
a boundary set by both Top/Dominant and bottom/submissive to define what each is willing and unwilling to do; applies to roles, levels of dominance and submission, time duration, and type and intensity of physical activities

**M/f**
an interaction and/or relationship in which the Top/Dominant is male and the bottom/submissive is female

**M/m**
an interaction and/or relationship in which both the Top/Dominant and the bottom/submissive are male

**Masochist**
one who derives sexual pleasure from pain

**Master**
how a male Dominant may choose to be addressed by his own submissive or slave; sometimes used as title such as Master Alex

**Mistress**
how a female Dominant may choose to be addressed by her own submissive or slave; sometimes used as title such as Mistress Betty

**Money Slave**
a slave whose primary purpose/fetish is to generate money for a Top/Dominant

**Munch**
    a regular social gathering in a public place, such as a restaurant or pub, of those who are interested in kink

**Negotiating a Scene**
    defining the parameters of what will occur within a specific period of time; used to determine how much power the bottom is granting the Top for the duration of the scene, what activities will be included, etc.

**Online Player**
    someone who claims to want a real life relationship but has no intention of ever meeting in person

**Owner**
    a person who has accepted symbolic ownership of a submissive or slave and the responsibility that goes with that

**Ownership Markings**
    permanent marks, such as brands or tattoos, that are symbols of the owned status of the submissive or slave

**PRICK**
    Personal Responsibility Informed Consensual Kink

**Pain Slut**
    someone with a high pain tolerance who is sexually stimulated by heavy degrees of pain

**Paraphilia**
    traits and behaviors involving nonstandard or unusual sexual interest and activities

**Party Service**
    someone who serves guests at parties, usually naked or in some type of fetish apparel

**Play**
    participate in bondage and/or S&M activities

**Player**
> someone who makes false claims to manipulate others

**Play Partner**
> someone with whom you participate in bondage and/or S&M activities

**Polyamory (also Poly)**
> intimate relationships that are not exclusive between two people

**ProDomme (aka Dominatrix)**
> a professional who tops according to the bottoms' desires/requests for specified periods of time, in exchange for financial compensation

**Property**
> an owned slave may be considered and/or treated as property as part of D/s dynamic

**Protocols**
> behavior standards that Dominants require their submissives to meet: clothing (or absence of) requirements, eye contact and speech restrictions, kneeling/genuflecting, etc.

**RACK**
> Risk Aware Consensual Kink

**RL or R/L (also RT)**
> Real Life or Real Time

**RACK**
> Risk Aware Consensual Kink

**Role Play**
> pretending to be someone/something else for the duration of a scene

**SSC**
> Safe Sane Consensual

**Sadist**
someone who derives sexual pleasure from inflicting pain
**Safeword**
a code word that a submissive can use to stop play when it becomes too painful or intense
**Scat**
feces; feces play
**Scene**
a defined period of time during which two or more people will exchange some level of power
**Scene Name**
a name chosen to use in the BDSM scene: may or may not include a title (such as Lady Alice, Sir Bob, or Slave Chris); may include a standard name, or a descriptive (such as Pixie, Dauphin, Bear), or consist of made up/foreign language terms
**Sissify**
forced cross-dressing and/or gender reassignment of a male submissive
**Sissy**
a male who adopts female clothing and/or mannerisms (sometimes exaggerated); most often straight
**Slave**
a submissive who has given themselves as property to an Owner
**Slave Contract**
a written agreement elaborating the terms, goals, and limits of a BDSM relationship
**Slave Registry**
a website set up to register slaves and assign them a unique number and bar code

**Squick(s)**
Something an individual finds repulsive, distasteful, creepy, revolting, etc. or something that freaks out that individual

**Submission**
a state of being submissive or compliant

**Submissive (also Sub)**
someone who surrenders (or wishes to surrender) the control of their body and behavior to a Dominant

**Subspace**
a drugged sensation bottoms can experience as a result of the endorphin rush induced by play; also can refer to the head space some submissives enter when in service

**Switch**
someone who enjoys both Top and bottom roles in BDSM play and/or someone who switches between domination and submission

**Top**
someone who takes the active role in a physical scene, but not necessarily emotional/mental control

**Top Drop**
an abrupt, temporary feeling of depression or unhappiness sometimes experienced by a Top immediately after a BDSM scene

**Topped/Topping from the bottom**
maintaining the fiction that the Top is in charge, when the bottom has the real control in the direction of a scene

**Topspace**
a drugged sensation Tops can experience as a result of the adrenalin rush induced by play

**Total Power Exchange (also TPE)**
a submissive granting authority to their Dominant to make all

decisions on their behalf in exchange for Dominant's agreement to take responsibility for their happiness and health

**Toybag**
a tote — ranging from large purse to steamer trunk — used to transport toys to events and/or play spaces

**Toys**
implements used in BDSM scene play

**Transgender**
an umbrella term, which usually includes individuals who identify as transsexuals, transvestites, genderqueer, gender fluid, intersex, and other gender variants

**Transsexual**
a person born with sexual characteristics of a gender that does not match their personal psychology; they often will go through gender reassignment by means of counseling, hormone treatments, and/or surgery

**Transvestite**
someone who dresses in the clothing of the opposite gender, sometimes in public and attempting to pass for that gender

**Vanilla**
used to describe anything that doesn't fall into kink/BDSM/fetish categories

**Watersports**
activities involving urine including drinking, golden showers, and wetting oneself

**WIITWD**
What It Is That We Do

**YKINMK**
Your Kink Is Not My Kink (usually followed by "but that's okay")

```
         Owner
        Dominant
           Top

         Switch
Sadist  Sadomasochist  Masochist
         Bottom

        Submissive
          Slave
```

# Chapter Three

## Labels

### BDSM Labels

*This essay originally appeared October 7, 2011 on BDSM Book Reviews.*

"How do you identify?" is a loaded question, no matter who's asking. The query can refer to your gender, sexual orientation, or role in the BDSM lifestyle. In all cases, binary or even ternary systems leave many people out and can create a great deal of confusion, especially online.

With one exception (to my knowledge) every BDSM networking site offers only three or four labels from which to choose: Dominant, submissive, switch, and possibly slave. This has made it difficult for those interested in learning more about kink to figure out their place in the spectrum because they have no clue what identities are possible. I know of one exception. Fetlife currently offers a more realistic 15 choices for BDSM role (and 12 each for gender and sexual orientation).

What follows is my opinion of what some labels mean. I don't hold myself out as an authority. But, I am a FemDom (and a top) and I own a submissive who lives in my home, serving me 24/7. I have spent a fair amount of time at various community events and also communicated with way too many online players. So for what it's worth …

**Domme**: This term created controversy (and also confusion about how it's pronounced). When I first signed onto Fetlife a few months after it went live, if you selected "female" and "dominant" you were automatically identified as a "Domme." This did not sit well with many. In general, the term refers to a female dominant as does

**FemDom**: Personally, I prefer FemDom because being a dominant female does present significant challenges in a patriarchal society and the dynamic of a F/m or F/f relationship tends (but isn't always) to be different than that of a M/f or M/m. Which brings us to:

**Dominatrix** is a professional who gets paid to top someone (usually male) in a BDSM scene. Often they're not dominants. They deliver what their clients want when it's wanted. Although their client may profess to be submissive, in reality, they're usually a

**Bottom**, someone who is a masochist or has other fetishes that puts them on the receiving end during a BDSM scene. Bottoms get bound, hurt, and/or humiliated, but they choose with whom they want to play and whatever form of play their scenes involve. They negotiate the level of restraint, pain, and degradation their scenes will include. Bottoms can use safewords to reduce the intensity level or stop the scene all together. The bottom's role ends when the scenes does, unlike a

**Submissive**: Online you can find endless lists of profiles in which the writers try to convince the reader how submissive they are using words like "well trained" and "obedient." Then they go on to describe how much they enjoy pain, bondage, and "punishment." A submissive is someone who serves, who cedes control of themselves and some or all aspects of their lives to their dominant in a relationship. Whereas bottoms ask tops to perform certain tasks for the bottoms' (and presumably the tops') pleasure, submissives enjoy serving their dominants' needs, even when that means performing tasks they would otherwise find onerous. The ultimate example is the submissive who is not a masochist, but who takes pain from their sadistic dominant only because the dominant enjoys hurting them. Depending on the relationship, submissives may not have safewords.

One can demonstrate submission during a scene. But, if one wants to be submissive in a Dominant/submissive (aka D/s) relationship, it works best if your partner(s) is a

**Dominant**: The key to domination is control. In D/s relationships, dominants make decisions about everything from what their submissive will wear and eat to whether and where they will work and play. How much control a dominant has can vary greatly and defines the relationship. The parties involved negotiate the level of control and type of relationship, but for months and years, not the few hours or days that a scene might last. If you're negotiating a scene, you're probably doing so with a

**Top**: In a BDSM scene, the top administers restraint, pain, and humiliation. But tops only deliver what the bottoms have requested and agreed to.

None of the definitions above are exclusive. One can be, for example, a dominant top (common), a dominant masochist (not so common), a submissive bottom, or a submissive top. A submissive who tops a masochistic dominant, delivering pain in exactly the way it's requested during a scene, may or may not be a

**Switch**, someone who can assume either role: top/bottom or dominant/submissive. Usually, the latter folks do not switch with the same person. They might be submissive to one person and dominant of another. Sadistic and masochistic (aka S&M) switches are more likely to change roles with the same person, although again some may only top different people than those they bottom to. Because switch can refer to either dominant/submissive or top/bottom, the term can become confusing so some folks prefer, in the latter case,

**Sadomasochist**, someone who enjoys both sadism and masochism. A

**Sadist** is often defined as someone who obtains pleasure from inflicting pain on others. However, that definition is missing a term. The word is derived from reference to stories about cruel sexual practices written by Count Donatien A.F. de Sade (who, despite modern references, was not a marquis). Paper dictionaries and psychiatric texts almost always include "sexual" in the definition. But online references often leave it out and many people claim not to find sexual gratification in certain S&M activities. Consensual sadism usually involves, on the receiving end, a

**Masochist**, referring to someone who gets sexual pleasure from being hurt or abused. The word derives from references to writing about bottoming sexually by Leopold von Sacher-Masoch (born more than two decades after de Sade died). Again, online references may omit the word "sexual" from the definition.

I'm not going to try to define Master or Mistress (which requires diving into gender politics). Many folks believe the terms can refer only those who own property. Others will claim they are such, regardless of their relationship status. Controversy around the term "slave" starts with how one differentiates between a slave and a submissive and includes disagreement over whether someone can claim to be a slave if they are not owned property.

Labels can confuse anyone, especially someone new to the lifestyle. One advantage of in-person over online interaction is that you're less likely to get trapped by a label that doesn't accurately define you, preventing you from wasting too much time corresponding with a dominant looking for a service submissive when you really just want a top who will blister your bottom.

# Chapter Four

## Dynamics

### What Some Women Tops and Bottoms Have in Common

*Winner National Leather Association — International Cynthia Slater Nonfiction Article Award, 2014*

*This essay originally appeared October 12, 2013 on BDSM Book Reviews*

Power dynamics have interesting implications. What some Doms do to control; others require their submissive to perform as a service.

When I had a convertible, I always drove my own car. I enjoyed the turbo charged engine and its ability to take curves at high speeds. I never let anyone else behind the wheel of that car, and my submissive rode with me as a passenger. But, when I traded my sports car in on a sedate sedan, the dynamic changed. Driving became boring, so now my submissive chauffeurs me. It's another way he serves me.

This implication can often be seen in D/s sexual interactions. When it comes to sex, women tops and bottoms often have something in common, besides the obvious. Although the context differs depending on their position in the D/s dynamic, many women abdicate the responsibility for their pleasure to their partners.

In some M/f relationships I've observed, the male puts a fair amount of effort into his submissive's orgasms, whether it's devising diabolical rape scenes or training her to come on voice command.

At the other end of the dynamic, some FemDoms expect their submissives to serve them by providing them with sexual pleasure — whether it's fetish-related such as foot worship or actual intercourse, often of the oral variety.

In either dynamic, the genitalia of the submissive may be considered owned by the Dominant. But, attitudes toward their possessions differ greatly.

In both cases, Dominants might enjoy tormenting their toys' sexual equipment. But, the male Dom may take pleasure in forcing his girl to come over and over again until she can't breathe while the FemDom asserts control by prohibiting her boy from having an orgasm.

This dichotomy is especially observable in chastity devices.

The male apparatus prevents him from having an erection and therefore, in most cases, an orgasm. The female restraint only obstructs penetration.

Now both top and bottom females may be very explicit about what they want, what arouses them, and what they find distasteful. And, of course the turn ons and offs are likely to be diametric opposites. But, even if they're very explicit about their likes and dislikes, many women prefer giving their partner control over whether or not, and how often, they come.

Personally, I can't comprehend why any woman would surrender her sexual pleasure to another, even if it's someone who works hard to satisfy her. I wonder if women do so because society considers female sexuality subservient to male's. Or are women hesitant to take control of their sexual pleasure because society dictates negative connotations for women who enjoy sex?

## It's Okay to Want to Bottom

One of the most difficult aspects of coming out as kinky, can be coming to terms with wanting to bottom. It's especially problematic for men. Our patriarchal society expects men to take charge, to be the head of the household, to make the decisions. Jokes abound about henpecked husbands and pussy whipped sissies.

But some men prefer it that way. Their job may demand that they take charge and make decisions, and at the end of the day they prefer to let a woman or another man assume control. Or they may be more comfortable serving than commanding. Or they may simply make the mistake of falling in love with a Dominant, and choose to submit to them because the Dominant won't tolerate any other type of relationship.

Even women who choose to submit get flack from so-called feminists who claim that BDSM practices "actively oppress women." (See Chapter 6.) Such claims are made by people with no knowledge or experience in BDSM.

The trick is to figure out what works for you. You may be a total Top, but meet someone who makes you want to bottom. (Or vice versa. In BDSM, there's always a vice versa and then something in between).

Some people might start at the bottom and later decide to become a switch, or even a Top. Or vice versa. I've seen both happen.

## Who Gets to Decide

There are people who define the D/s dynamic strictly by gender. Female supremacists believe only females should be Dominant. Patriarchy participants and many evangelicals are convinced that all men should be in charge.

But, they're both wrong. I've known women who couldn't dominate a flea and others (including myself) whom no man could successfully dominate. Ditto men.

The continuum of domination and submission is very fluid, and personal. One person of a specific gender may make you want to drop to your knees while another of that same gender may inspire you to bring out the figurative whip. Or you may only submit to women while always dominating men. And then there's the Dominant who meets someone more Dominant who chooses to submit to that Dominant because they want to be involved with that person.

The most important thing to remember is *no one else* gets to decide your orientation. If a male female supremacist insists you should dominate him because you're a woman, but you only want to bottom, ignore him. Ditto if a male patriarchy participant orders you to submit because you're female. You are perfectly within your rights to tell them to go to hell or block them (or both).

If you're confused about where you fall in the spectrum, take your time figuring out where you belong and to what extent and under what circumstances, if any, you want to switch orientation. You may incline toward dominance on Tuesday and submission on Friday. Doesn't matter. Although you might want to identify as a switch, no one else gets to choose your identity for you. Any attempt to do so qualifies as abuse.

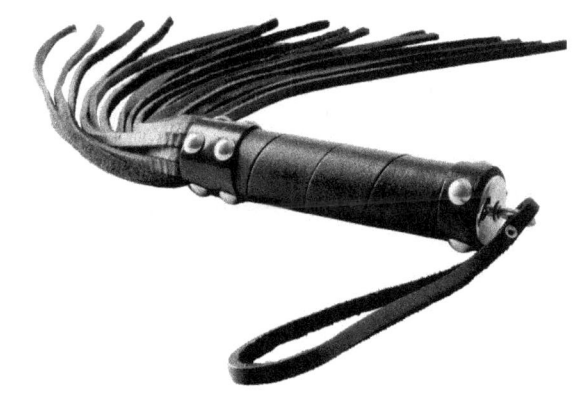

# Chapter Five
## Fantasy vs Reality

### Fiction vs Fact

Fiction paints all kinds of interesting pictures about what it's like to live the BDSM lifestyle.

In Laura Antoniou's *Marketplace* series, for example, perfect slaves are trained to be perfect for buyers who will offer them a life of perfect slavery. In *Exit to Eden* by Anne Rampling (aka Anne Rice), would-be slaves sail to an idyllic island where they participate in sex contests for the amusement of the rich and powerful. In Cecilia Tan's *Struck by Lightning* series, a wealthy businessman plucks a waitress from her meaningless existence and introduces her to the exotic world of pain for pleasure. In K.D.

Grace's The *Pet Shop,* human pets are dispatched from a private kennel to entertain and fuck.

Great reads all. My descriptions are deliberately flippant because all of these books are fictional. (You can look up the real blurbs for better representation of what the stories are about.) Enjoy reading them, but understand you will never find those situations, settings, and people in real life.

Which doesn't stop folks from fantasizing about being put on the auction block or delivered with collar and food bowl to a beautiful owner for the weekend or meeting someone filthy rich who will rescue them from their life struggles and keep them imprisoned on their luxurious mansion.

In reality, we all live in a vanilla world, and most of us have to go to work every day.

Gorgeous, skinny FemDoms don't spend their time mincing about in corsets and six-inch heels. Not all of us are magazine cover models. Many of us find spiked heels unpleasant and hard to walk in. And corsets are restrictive and uncomfortable.

Muscular, rich male Dominants don't swagger about all day in leather chaps, boots, and vests. Some of them are short and stout and work in a service position. Leather doesn't cut it for daily wear, especially if you have a job that requires a suit or uniform or coveralls to protect your clothing from grease or paint.

Slaves don't run around naked on multi-acre estates or spend their days in cages or shackled to the wall. For one thing, if you're in a cage, then someone has to take care of *you.* (You can't be left alone safely, you'll need food and other things.) That requires that the person who put you in the cage or locked you up serves you, not the other way around.

## Online Advantages

Be careful about dragging fantasies out of your head into the real world. Something that seems really hot when you're jerking off, might terrify you in real life.

A major advantage of online play is that it allows you to *pretend* to do things you might not want to try in person.

However, one disadvantage of online play is that if you try to take that really hot fantasy offline, it might be painful. I've known people who got exactly what they thought they wanted, then turned tail and ran when they discovered that their fantasy didn't work in the real world. They learned that the whip actually stings when it hits their naked buttocks, or that their tongue and jaw got tired when they attempted to deliver oral sex as long as the Top wanted it.

## Submissives ≠ Doormats

Some people, especially online, seem to believe that they have the right to demand servility and obedience from anyone they find attractive who identifies as a submissive. And some who identify as submissives are under the *mistaken* notion that they should deliver on demand.

But submissives are not doormats. They are precious and should be cherished, their service rewarded, their devotion returned.

In most cases, "submissive" should only apply if it's following a possessive pronoun or noun, e.g., "my submissive" or "Lady

T's submissive." Although it may not be their nature, submissives choose to submit to specific persons, hopefully someone they love. Submission should be reserved for those who have captured their heart and earned their surrender.

Submissives should never be expected to kneel before anyone just because that person presents as a Dominant. A submissive is not someone in service to any person who snaps their fingers.

## Submission is Not For Sale

Submission cannot be bought. If the first thing someone asks you for is money, they're not a "Dominant," they're a grifter. Someone who claims to be a "Dominant," but who demands tribute before they will even communicate with you, is just a scam artist.

## Service ≠ Submission

Also be aware that service does not equal submission. You can serve someone — cleaning their house, washing their car, giving them a massage, running their errands, serving them sexually — without submitting to them. A Dominant must earn your submission and it takes time to develop the trust that's required to give them your submission.

## Submission is Not a Gift

One statement I hear frequently, from both online and real-life practitioners, is that submission is a gift from the submissive to the Dominant.

I disagree. If you give someone a gift, it should be given freely with no strings attached. The recipient is not even obligated to use the gift, although in polite society, at least a thank you is required.

Submission comes with a whole cobweb of responsibilities and obligations. It and the person giving it should be honored. They should be respected. But, submission should *never* be given without expectations of something in return.

# Chapter Six
## BDSM vs abuse

### Not All of Us Are Damaged, but Predators Are Very Real

The kink community population most likely includes the same percentage as any other slice of society of people who had terrible childhoods, were victims of abuse, and/or suffer from depression or other mental illnesses. We are *not* broken people seeking therapy through the giving or receiving of pain. That said, we also have predators among us, just like any other community.

Unfortunately, taking advantage of a new submissive can be very easy for an abuser, as seen in the *Fifty Shades of Grey* series of books and movie. By exposing a masochist to subspace and hooking them on that euphoria, a clever abuser can have them eating out of their hands and committed to a twisted version of a D/s relationship before the submissive can come up for air. There are major differences between a healthy D/s relationship and an abusive relationship of any kind, be it kinky or vanilla.

# Avoiding Abuse in the Search for D/s

*This essay originally appeared April 30, 2012*
*on BDSM Book Reviews*

Sometimes, only a thin line separates BDSM from abuse in a relationship. Especially online, you find people who claim that their "naturally dominant" personalities entitle them to demand submission of others: to take ownership of mind, body, and soul. The only thing creepier than Dominants who profess their superiority are the submissives who offer themselves up for this sort of abuse.

True, many submissives simply echo the erotic fantasies that haunt them, reciting the words they've seen others type, reiterating what they see in online porn. Most shun real-time opportunities. Although a few may go so far as to present themselves for service, reality and pain soon send them back to the comfort of their online world. But some actually put themselves in the hands of the those who have no education, little experience, and less understanding of the responsibilities that come with accepting someone's submission.

I especially worry about the submissives who have low (or no) self-esteem, who think enslavement will solve their vanilla-world problems, who make decisions based on the reaction between their legs instead of the one between their ears. They get damaged — emotionally, physically, and financially.

"I am dominant by nature and like to be in control," more than one profile claims. They makes no reference to experience, knowledge, or caring for a submissive. "I am a True Master seeking a true sub/slave to serve Me," another common declaration. Exactly what does that mean?

BDSM organizations have defined abuse as: "Physical, sexual, or emotional acts inflicted on a person without their informed and freely given consent."

But without training and experience, without care and consideration, abuse can happen even with consent. Someone who consents to a D/s relationship without prior knowledge of what it involves or the person to whom he/she is submitting is a perfect candidate for emotional abuse. This statement, in a "slave's" online journal, speaks volumes about what the person writing it has experienced in the past. "i need some security and to feel good that i am not going to be thrown away for a simple reason."

That boi consented to a D/s relationship. He offered himself as a slave to someone who professed experience and presented a "leather resume" that was, for the most part fabricated. What he didn't get from the Dominant to whom he gave himself was references from others who had served him. The emotional abuse that ensued took its toll, and it required the better part of a year for the boi to heal from a month-long enslavement.

To work, a Dominant/submissive relationship must offer symbiotic benefits to everyone involved. Even a slave should ask: "What's in it for me?" Dominants who do not ensure that their submissives' needs get met, as well as their own, do not deserve the title of Master/Mistress. Those who abuse their submissives — who don't respect and treasure them as human beings — give all a bad name.

Friendship, love, intimacy, respect, and trust form the core of all relationships. Without any one of those, the connection between two (or more) people will not last. The strongest D/s relationships I know are the ones that started out as two people in love. Often the D/s aspect grew organically out of their love affair/marriage. Their unions have endured for decades. However, those who seek Owners or slaves without developing deeper relationships, most likely will not survive together a year.

One can meet one's soul mate online. I know a number of couples/families who have done so, including those who started out geographically very far apart. And it helps if you share common interests in S&M and D/s, so seeking that soul mate on a site for alternative lifestyles offers advantages. But, look beyond the labels and see the person. Get to know the man or woman on many levels before venturing into a Master/slave contract. D/s demands incredible trust. You cannot achieve trust without scrupulous honesty, and that requires a lot of communication.

The best way to avoid abuse is to take precautions from the moment you meet a potential new partner. I highly recommend Jack Rinella's book *Partners in Power*. Not only does he address safety, but he also talks about types of real-world relationships and what it takes to find the right partner and actually make a D/s relationships work.

If you got involved in a relationship without taking precautions, if you allowed fantasies and desire to overrule common sense, it's critical that you be honest with yourself now. Anyone who suspects they (or someone they care about) has suffered from abuse, needs to ask these questions (developed at Leather Leadership Conference in 1999):

"1.   Are your needs and limits respected?

"2.   Is your relationship built on honesty, trust, and respect?

"3.   Are you able to express feelings of guilt or jealousy or unhappiness?

"4.   Can you function in everyday life?

"5.   Can you refuse to do illegal activities?

"6.   Can you insist on safe sex practices?

"7.   Can you choose to interact freely with others outside of your relationship?

"8.   Can you leave the situation without fearing that you will be harmed, or fearing the other participant(s) will harm themselves?

"9.   Can you choose to exercise self-determination with money, employment, and life decisions?

"10.   Do you feel free to discuss your practices and feelings with anyone you choose?"

If any of those questions generates a "No" answer, the relationship is potentially abusive. You can find help by contacting the

National Leather Association — International Domestic Violence Project at http://www.nlaidvproject.us, your local domestic violence hotline, or the National Domestic Violence Hotline at 1-800-799-SAFE (7233) or http://www.ndvh.org/

Stay safe.

# Erotic Power Exchange vs Abuse

*This rest of this chapter is distilled from*
Using Power Exchange to Enhance Your Sexual Relationships,
*a program I have given on several occasions*

Erotic Power Exchange requires *voluntary, informed, consent given by adults who are not impaired in any way.* Anything that occurs outside of that definition can be considered abuse.

## Abuse Can Occur When:

- ✧ Consent is not voluntary and given of one's own free will.
- ✧ The activities did not occur between adults who are mentally able to give consent.
- ✧ An activity is not voluntarily and mutually agreed upon *ahead* of time by the participants.
- ✧ The consent was given under the influence of drugs, alcohol, emotional duress, physical stress, or anything else that would impede or preclude one's ability to give consent.
- ✧ The activities were the result of any form of coercion, exploitation, or fear of reprisal that may have been utilized to obtain consent.
- ✧ Consent was previously withdrawn.

## Signs to Watch For:

- ✧ Are you afraid of your partner?
- ✧ Do you worry about blackmail?
- ✧ Does your partner ridicule you for the limits you set?
- ✧ Do you feel obliged to participate in sexual acts?
- ✧ Does your partner isolate you from friends and family or stop you from participating in activities?
- ✧ Are you or your partner emotionally dependent on one another?
- ✧ Does your relationship swing back and forth between emotional distance and closeness?
- ✧ Does your partner constantly criticize or humiliate you and undermine your self esteem?
- ✧ Do you feel you cannot discuss what is bothering you with your partner?
- ✧ Are you confused about when a scene begins and ends?
- ✧ Does your partner ignore your safewords or pressure you not to use them?
- ✧ Has your partner ever violated your limits?
- ✧ Has your partner ever attempted to expand negotiations *during* a scene?
- ✧ Do you feel trapped in a specific role (submissive or Dominant)?
- ✧ Does your partner use scenes to express or cover up anger and frustration?

# VS

# Chapter Seven
## Staying Safe Online

### Guarding Your Privacy Online

If you log onto any fetish or social media site, you are liable to see the following message (or something similar) on various profiles:

*WARNING: Any institutions or individuals using this site or any of its associated sites for studies or projects, profit or nonprofit projects — You DO NOT have my permission to use any of my profile or pictures in any form or forum both current and future. You may not cut, copy, paste anything from/off my profile including photos, videos and/or writings in any way, shape or form. If you have or do, it will be considered a violation of my privacy and will be subject to legal ramifications.*

Be aware this warning is meaningless. It's not a legally binding statement. The legal document you signed, by accepting the TOS (terms of service) when setting up a profile on *any* site, trumps anything you post and probably says pretty much the opposite.

The most important thing to understand when creating an account on any website that is free (and even some that charge a fee) is that you're not the consumer, you're the *product*.

Now, on Facebook and other conventional social media sites, the most embarrassing thing anyone else might learn about you is somewhat limited by the restrictions the site has on what you can post.

But, sites like Fetlife and Collarspace have no such restrictions. And the product is no longer just your gossip and cute pictures of your pets. It's your sex life.

## I've Seen That Face Before

Unless you can afford being outed as a kinkster, don't post naked pictures of yourself in bondage with whip marks on your ass if they also show your face, tattoos, piercings, or other identifiable body modifications recognizable to anyone else who might stumble across them ... or go looking for them. Don't use pictures that show identifiable backgrounds, or that you may have also uploaded to a conventional social media site or to a website connected with your legal name. Check the background. Can you read the certificate perhaps showing your legal name that you hang on your bedroom wall?

A website that requires you to log on offers *nothing* to make you or your identity safe. Don't believe that no one can see your photographs unless they're also logged in. And don't believe any promises of privacy offered by a site, because they're not accurate.

For one thing, anyone can create a free email account on any one of a dozen sites while providing no information that can be traced back to them. They can then use that email address to create an account on the site you think is protecting you from non-kinksters' eyes.

Further, those photographs can be accessed without logging in. Fetish sites are often free or partially free. They don't invest money in security that protects the content. And there's no guarantee that if you post a photograph that you'll ever be able to delete it. Even if it is removed from a site, it's probably still in the cloud storage system used by that site and therefore recoverable by anyone who knows what they're doing. People have had deleted, "private" photos they posted online used against them in court.

If the photo you posted was taken with your smartphone, chances are the file contains data about where and when it was taken and other information that can be used to identify you.

Combine all these security holes with facial recognition software (which can deliver matches even when years, facial hair, weight, and makeup change someone's appearance) and you have a recipe for disaster. What would happen if your boss found the picture of you getting gang banged or the private detective hired by your ex who's fighting you for custody of your children turned up a photograph of you hanging naked and upside down in bondage or a prospective employer discovered images of you whipping someone chained to a rack?

Online privacy is almost nonexistent. I've always said that you should never post anything online that you wouldn't want your boss, your elderly grandmother, your worst enemy, and the IRS to see — or at least don't post it if there's any way it can be traced back to you.

## Play at Your Own Risk

*This essay originally appeared April 13, 2010 on my blog*

I am constantly amazed by how willing people are to expose themselves to potential harm because someone makes it sound like fun. Most recently, I saw a rash of updates on Twitter stating "Just took 'Which Crazy Writer Are You?' and got: _____" which was, of course, posted with a link so others could try it.

I checked out the quiz and discovered that after you answer all the question, in order to get any results, you must hand over your Twitter user name *and* password. Why in the world would anyone do that? How do they know what the quiz creator will do with that information? (I got a clue about what the quiz creator intended later when I saw apologies along the lines of "Sorry if the 'Crazy Writer' quiz spammed everyone" accompanied by claims that they "didn't realize it would do that.")

No one creates Twitter quizzes, Facebook games, and applications such as Foursquare because they want to entertain you for free. They're in it for money and they're using *your* data to get it.

For example, every time you sign up for a Facebook game, you give the developer of that application permission to access ALL of your personal data, including your "private" emails.

Facebook stripped away almost all pretense of privacy (while claiming to enhance it), when it changed default settings to make anything posted on Facebook public unless the poster goes to great lengths to keep the information private. Many categories of information — including your name, profile photo, list of friends and fan pages, gender, geographic region, and applications — no longer even have privacy options.

If you choose to lock your Twitter page to "protect" your tweets, your followers can still retweet them. Your tweets show up on Google searches of your name. The United States Library of Congress is archiving *every* single tweet.

At least one man believes his home was burglarized as a result of announcements about his vacation to his Twitter followers. The whole point of foursquare.com, as far as I can tell, is to tell everyone, via Twitter, where you are at any given moment, leaving yourself vulnerable to stalkers and burglars. Even those who don't participate in Foursquare, are urged by Twitter to add their location to each tweet.

The Internet Patrol warns: "There is an inherent problem – dare we even say it – danger – with letting the world know where you are or, even, where you aren't.

"For example, do you really want some Twitter whacko stalking you at your place of employment? Or following you to a restaurant? Or even to your home?"

Scambusters warns that "you should be aware of the amount and type of information you're giving out that can be used against you."

Insurance companies are demanding access to online information about you *without* your explicit consent. Creditors and prospective employers are checking out your Facebook and Twitter accounts.

People have gotten fired, lost opportunities for employment, and had their disability benefits taken away because of Facebook posts. Businesses have had brands and goodwill destroyed by Twitter campaigns (sometimes deservedly). Personally, I have stopped following many of those on my Facebook friends' list, because while I might want to know if they sold a story or won an award, I have no interest in reading about their activities on FarmVille, Candy Crush, etc.

Certainly, if you choose to hand over your passwords and other personal information to unknown developers, that's your prerogative. Just don't be surprised, or complain, when that data is used against you.

## General Safety Protocols

There are safety precautions you should take anywhere online, so I'm just going to list them. If you're not sure how to do any of these, you can find more information with a quick web search.

- ✧ Use long (12-character minimum) passwords with at least one capital letter, one numeral, and one symbol.
- ✧ Do not use the same password for any two sites, especially if

one of those sites is kinky and/or has access to your financial data.
- Protect your passwords, do not write them down on paper. There are myriad password tracking applications you can install on your hard drive to manage them all.
- Change your passwords regularly.
- Do not use an email address that has your name in it (or is attached in any way to your contact list) to log onto a fetish site.
- Do not log onto a fetish site on a public computer or via a public wireless connection. The filter may lock you out. Even if doesn't, your activity can be monitored by a system administrator and associated with the information you used to log in to the network, such as your library card number or your computer's MAC address.
- Do not log into a fetish site from your phone if you're using your name and/or an email address that can be traced to you on that device.
- If you share your computer with someone else, especially minors, delete your history, cache, and cookies each time you let them use the machine.
- Never give your password to anyone else.

## Staying Safe Emotionally

If you haven't read Chapter 6 (BDSM vs abuse), I recommend you do so, even if you're never planning to meet someone in real life. It's possible to suffer abuse online as well as in person, especially emotional abuse.

Online, you will find people who claim that they are entitled to demand your submission right out of the gate. They will insist they should be allowed to take ownership of your mind, body, and soul — even if you've never met. They will demand you address them as "Master" or "Mistress" in early email exchanges, require that you obey their orders, and not allow you to correspond with anyone else without their permission. They might ask you to announce on your profile that you're under consideration or owned by them. And they might insist you give them your password for the site.

These are *all* warning signs of an abuser.

## Playing Online

If you want to play games with someone you've met online, go for it. But, you should never accept ownership/control (especially financial) from someone you have never met. Make sure you enjoy the sessions you have — otherwise why bother?

Some basic guidelines for staying safe if you play online:

- Don't do anything that makes you uncomfortable.
- Don't send a face photograph, *especially* not via the fetish site. (Remember, there is no such thing as "private" email.)
- Don't send a photograph of anything else that distinguishes you, such as a tattoo or birthmark or distinctive piercings.
- If you play via webcam, make sure the cam is pointing to an area of your room that has no distinguishing features or information. Take a picture first to check the camera's range. (Again, avoid showing your face or anything else that distin-

guishes you, such as a tattoo or birthmark or distinctive piercings.)
- ✧ Don't share your physical address, phone number, or other information that would allow you to be found in the real world.
- ✧ Don't reveal details about where you work or any organizations you belong to.
- ✧ Get a throwaway cell phone or a Google voice phone number for voice conversations. Better yet, use a VoIP application (such as Skype) attached to the same email address you use on the fetish site.
- ✧ Don't make yourself susceptible to blackmail (emotional or financial) by sharing too much information about your personal life.

# Chapter Eight
## The Numbers

### So Many Men

On dating websites, males often significantly outnumber females. For fetish sites, I've heard numbers that range from between three to ten men for every one woman. Some of those women are actually men pretending to be female. (In this case, I'm not referring to transgender women, but to men who *claim* to be female for various reasons, such as to get lesbian women to converse with them or to act out their fantasies with men who believe they are corresponding with a female.)

Males, even submissive males, operate from a position of cultural privilege — one they rarely recognize and often deny. A female's best defense against male behavior she considers abusive, is the website's blocking function. (And it doesn't matter what he believes — if his behavior makes her uncomfortable in any way, it's abusive.)

If you are a male contacting a female online, don't assume that a female, either submissive or Dominant, owes you *anything*. If you want to avoid getting blocked, remember:

## Just Because

- ✧ you write to her, doesn't obligate her to respond. (In fact, if you don't approach her the way she's requested in her profile or if you're outside the parameters she's specified, she's not even obligated to read your email before she blocks you.)
- ✧ she asks you a question and you answer it, doesn't obligate her to continue corresponding.
- ✧ you and she corresponded, doesn't obligate her to meet with you.
- ✧ you express a desire to treat her to dinner, doesn't obligate her to accept.
- ✧ she has more experience than you and you have questions about BDSM, doesn't obligate her to educate you.
- ✧ she refuses to correspond, meet, or educate you, that doesn't make her "mean."

And, if any of the above statements do engender "she's so mean" or similar thoughts from you, you are moving from your male privilege into male asshole/bully territory.

# Why Women are Demanding Online

One of the ways women combat privileged male bullies is by being *very* specific on their profiles about how they want to be approached, what parameters they consider essential before they will correspond, and what they will and will not do.

That makes it easier for them to wade through all the inappropriate messages. The younger and more attractive a woman is, the more she will get inundated by email from clueless males, wannabees, do me bottoms, online players, fantasy boys, and guys looking to cheat on their wives.

If you're a male approaching a female online, you will not get *any* benefit of the doubt. If you don't want to get blocked right out of the gate, you need to prove to her that you're different. (And you can't do that by just saying so, you have to show her.)

- Read her profile carefully before you email her.
- Respond respectfully to what she has written.
- Follow her directions if she lists them.
- Provide her any information she's requested.
- Be polite and specific, don't deluge her with vague, meaningless platitudes.
- Spell/grammar check your words before you hit send.

If you do these things, you'll stand out from the crowd and probably get a response, even if you're not exactly what she seeks. These tactics also will significantly increase the likelihood that you'll find what you're looking for.

# Chapter Nine

## Staying Safe if You Venture Out

### Guarding Your Privacy

Essentially, you have three options for protecting your identity when you get involved in kink in real life:

#### Anonymity

The ultimate protection — also the most difficult to maintain if you ever want to attend any events — is complete anonymity. It requires putting absolutely no identifying information about yourself anywhere that it can be used against you. That includes not posting any pictures that someone might guess are of you.

Thinking about getting into politics, going into social services, adopting a child, or working for the government? This is definitely the choice for you.

## Alter Ego

Alternatively, you could create an alter ego using a different name, email address, etc. The more you become involved in the kink community, the more you may choose to add to that identity. It's not that difficult, for example, to get a credit card in an alter ego's name. Identification is more problematic, however, and you probably will have to reveal your legal name in order to gain entrance into the many events that must ask for proof of age. Those records are supposed to be kept secure and private. But —

A post office box provides you with an alternative mailing address, but you won't be able to get one without identification, so again that's an organization that knows both of your identities.

## Out in the Open

For some, complete transparency is an option. Then you can post all the identifiable photographs you want. And you don't have to remember who knows which of your personas or worry about someone finding out about your kink and blabbing to your boss/spouse/ex/mother. But, you need to think long and hard about this option. Be prepared to live with it, forever. With the first two options, there's always a risk of someone finding out. The latter choice, on this planet connected by the World Wide Web, means that you've told the entire globe just who you are.

## Avoiding Predators

The myth that you can check on someone's references to avoid predators *only* serves to provide a false sense of security. It doesn't take into account that people can be afraid to say anything bad about someone who's abused them, because that person still has some power over them. It doesn't take into account that the community will protect someone who holds positions of authority in organizations — especially if they own dungeon space — even if that person has been accused of abuse.

To avoid potential libel lawsuits, fetish sites won't allow you to post derogatory information about someone without a court conviction, ignoring how difficult it may be to have someone arrested for abuse. In the vanilla world, any woman courageous enough to bring rape charges is treated as a criminal and re-victimized by the police and the court system. Imagine how much more difficult it would be to prosecute a rape case if the victim consented to some (but not all) of the "perverted" activities engaged in. Also, filing a complaint creates a public record that allows your abuser to learn your name, address, and other contact information. Some people can't risk anyone knowing about their kink activities, a fact that predators often use to their advantage.

## How Do You Protect Yourself?

- ✧ Trust your instincts. If something makes you feel uncomfortable, back away.
- ✧ Ask questions. Lots of questions. Judge the person responding

not just based on their answers, but also their attitude. If some of your questions cause the person you're questioning to get defensive, if they claim you shouldn't ask that or you should just trust them, back away.

⬥ Express your needs. What do you want out of the relationship? If the response is "I'm the Dominant, your needs don't matter" or "I'm the Dominant, I'll decide what you need," back away.

⬥ If you do check references, ask open-ended questions and try to get the person you're questioning to confide in you. Listen to what isn't said. If they give a glowing report, ask if they know anyone else who might have been involved with that person.

⬥ Don't give anyone money, buy them a plane ticket, purchase gifts for them, or pay their bills, unless they're a professional and you're paying for session time. (The exception, of course, is if your kink is to give someone money and get nothing in return.)

# Meeting in Person

⬥ Whenever possible, meet someone new for the first time at a gathering, such as a munch or an event. This has two advantages: you're less likely to be attacked and if they're a no-show you've something else to do.

⬥ Play with someone at a party before you go to their home or bring them to yours.

⬥ If you go on a blind date or go to play with someone at their home, always make sure a friend knows where you are and checks up on you. Just giving them the name and address of where you're going isn't enough. Set a check-in time and inform your date that if you don't call in or answer your phone by the specified time, your friend will call the authorities. Better to be embarrassed by the cops showing up because you forgot to call, than to have them only know where to start looking for your body.

When I used to go on blind dates, I would have a trusted friend call my cell at several intervals until I gave her an all-clear signal. That also gave me a way to extricate myself from an uncomfortable situation. I would simply turn the call into my friend's "emergency" plea for help and apologize because I had to go "rescue" them.

# Chapter Ten

## Understanding Erotic Power Exchange

*This chapter is distilled from*
Using Power Exchange to Enhance Your Sexual Relationships,
*a program I have given on several occasions*

To the uninformed, erotic power exchange can look like the mindset that feminists have fought against for decades. But feminism is also about choice. No one should be forced into any role because of their plumbing. Neither should anyone be prevented, because of their gender, from giving up control if they choose to do so.

Erotic power exchange requires that someone consent to ceding control over some facet of his or her life for some period of time to someone else. Yes, I am being deliberately vague. That's because the range of options is almost infinite: from allowing your date to choose where you will eat dinner without consulting you, to giving your partner control over every aspect of your daily life. And there's a huge variety of choices in between.

Since online S&M has some serious shortcomings and not everyone enjoys pain, one of the most popular forms online kink takes is erotic power exchange. One partner gives another some level of control for a specified period of time during which some form of sexual interaction may or may not take place.

Of course we must keep in mind that what each of us finds sexually satisfying can vary greatly. I have literally beaten a woman to orgasm, just for one example. Some folks find sucking on toes, or having their toes sucked, sexually thrilling. Others get turned on by sharing their sexual fantasies via telephone, email, chat, or VoIP. But this book is not here to define what constitutes sex.

Erotic power exchange, in and of itself, can be a turn on. Some people just find it exciting to take control or let someone else take control. If you work in a position where you're making decisions all day, it can be a great stress release to turn decision making over to your partner even for only a few hours. On the other hand, if your job leaves you feeling powerless, taking control of your partner for an evening can help you cope.

None of us choose what turns us on. Nor do we choose with whom we fall in love. We can decide whether or not we want to *act* on any sexual attraction — but we can no more choose whether or not we find the same or opposite sex (or both) attractive, than we can choose whether or not kneeling, or putting a partner on their knees, makes us hot. So, if you and your long-term partner, or the person you've been corresponding with online, get turned on by erotic power exchange, the first required step is to negotiate the terms of that power exchange.

## One Size Does Not Fit All

It's important to remember that in erotic power exchange (as in any aspect of BDSM), one size does not fit all. One person's hottest fantasy is another's biggest turn off. You must figure out:

- what turns you on;
- what turns you off;
- what turns your partner on;
- what turns your partner off; and
- where you and your partner can meet in the middle if any of those parameters are very far apart.

Obviously it's easy if one partner gets off on pretending to be a cop and the other a prisoner the cop is interrogating. It can be harder if one partner wants to try watersports, while just thinking about that makes the other partner nauseous. In that case, you'll need to find a way to compromise, perhaps by *pretending* to do something rather than actually doing it — which is always a good option when the relationship is online.

In the case where a person gets turned on by an activity that leaves their partner cold, it may work better if they do that activity with a different person — which is how many folks end up looking online *even* when they're in a committed relationship. If someone has no interest in that activity and is not comfortable with their partner having a real life encounter, online provides that partner an option.

## To Cheat or Not to Cheat, That is the Question

Depending on how you define the parameters of your real life relationship, and what activities you participate in with your online companion, your primary partner could embrace the philosophy that it doesn't matter where you get your appetite as long as you come home for dinner. However, you still need to be honest with both your primary partner and your online playmate.

The dictionary defines a cheat as someone "who acts dishonestly, deceives, or defrauds." If everyone involved knows about everyone else, you're not a cheater. When you're open and honest with your partner, and your online BDSM interactions get you all excited, they'll welcome your desire to have hot naked monkey sex afterwards.

On the other hand, if you don't inform your partner about your online activities, you're less likely to be able to benefit from any in-person interaction inspired by your online erotic power exchange.

I'm not going to get into the pros, cons, or logistics of polyamory here — you can find entire books on the subject. But erotic power exchange can spice up your sex life, even if both partners aren't involved in the same activities or with each other. And you can bring in other play partners but still remain monogamous in terms of actual sexual intercourse, if that's your preference.

Even if you don't believe you can share your BDSM fantasies with your real-life partner, at least be honest with your online playmate. They should know that you have a primary whom you have no interest in leaving. People can and do fall in love long distance. Save the pain and heartache of that, by being up-front about the extent of what you offer.

# Limits and Boundaries

Limits and boundaries are fluid and will change as you discover more about yourself sexually. But I recommend that in the beginning you set the boundaries closer in rather than farther out. It's easy to expand boundaries. It's much, much harder to narrow them.

Moving from erotic power exchange to incorporating domination and submission into your relationship takes your limits to an entirely new level. Again, that can range from making decisions about what someone will eat and wear and how they'll behave when they're with you, to taking control of every aspect of their life in what is called a total power exchange relationship.

D/s is not a relationship structure you should attempt to invoke the first time you try erotic power exchange, and if an online playmate wants to go there, that's a warning signal.

An erotic power exchange that lasts for only a few hours requires significant trust and communication. Turning your life over to a Dominant — or taking complete responsibility for another's life and well-being — requires much, much more trust and communication. In either case, the Dominant, or the Top, must earn the respect, trust, and submission of the bottom or the submissive. The reverse is also true. The bottom/submissive must earn the respect, trust, and dominance of the Top/Dominant.

It is, of course, much easier to develop enough trust to allow an exchange of power for a few hours online, than it is to develop enough trust to give someone real life TPE-level control. But without trust, respect, and consent, *any* level of erotic power exchange can cross over the line and become abuse. (See Chapter 6.)

# Where Do You Start?

I would recommend you begin by having a conversation with yourself. Admit your deep dark fantasies (and try to set aside any intellectual reservations) *before* you bring them to your partner or try to find someone to participate with you. This may require that you to do some research. And for some folks, learning that they are not the only one who wants to dress up in pigtails and pinafores and get seduced by their "mommy," or have their partner shave their legs and suck their toes, can make their fantasies less inhibiting.

If you are in a committed relationship, your next step should be to sit down with your partner and talk about things you would like to try. Now that may be a long list or a short one. If it's a long one, don't attempt to discuss everything all at once. Pick something that really appeals to you or that you think your partner will enjoy. And it's probably best to start with something simple.

For example, if you fantasize about three dykes kidnapping you, throwing you on the back of a Hog, and carrying you off to the woods where they molest you for days, you might want to save that one until you have had some experience. A scene that complicated will require careful planning and logistical expertise. You do not want to end up like the couple who had their play rape scene interrupted by the police because a homeless woman thought it was real and called 911.

(See Chapter 11 for negotiating what will be allowed to happen between partners and/or playmates.)

When you do start trying things, don't be disappointed if your first attempt squicks you out or you both crack each other up and end up with stomach cramps from laughing too hard. The important thing is to open your mind to other approaches to interacting with people. Even if you find your fantasy doesn't play well outside your head, you will benefit from having explored it.

| Activity | 5 really enjoy | 4 enjoy a little | 3 don't enjoy, but can tolerate | 2 not ready for that but perhaps in the future | 1 hard limit no | Experienced in the past | No Experience |
|---|---|---|---|---|---|---|---|
| 24/7 Total Power Exchange | | | | | | | |
| Anal Sex (with a man) | | | | | | | |
| Ass Worship (Giving) | | | | | | | |
| Biting | | | | | | | |
| Blindfolds | | | | | | | |
| Bondage | | | | | | | |
| Branding | | | | | | | |
| Candle Wax | | | | | | | |
| Chains | | | | | | | |
| Chastity Devices | | | | | | | |
| Chastity Piercings | | | | | | | |
| Clamps | | | | | | | |
| Cock and Ball Torture | | | | | | | |
| Collar and Lead/Leash | | | | | | | |
| Confinement/Caging | | | | | | | |
| Creampie cleanup | | | | | | | |
| Cuckolding | | | | | | | |
| Depilation/Shaving | | | | | | | |
| Deprivation (food, sleep, movement, sensory) | | | | | | | |
| Dildos/Plugs (hand held/strap on) | | | | | | | |
| Discipline | | | | | | | |
| Domestic/Public Servitude | | | | | | | |
| Electrotorture (EMS TENS units, etc.) | | | | | | | |
| Feathers / tickling | | | | | | | |
| Fire Play | | | | | | | |
| Floggers | | | | | | | |
| Foot Worship (giving) | | | | | | | |
| Hair Pulling | | | | | | | |
| Handcuffs/Shackles | | | | | | | |
| Humiliation / forced feminization | | | | | | | |
| Knife Play | | | | | | | |
| Massage (giving) | | | | | | | |
| Nipple Torture, Clamps, etc. | | | | | | | |
| No-Strings Housework | | | | | | | |
| Objectification | | | | | | | |
| Oral sex (giving – female) | | | | | | | |
| Oral sex (giving – male) | | | | | | | |
| Pain | | | | | | | |
| Piercings | | | | | | | |
| Pinching | | | | | | | |
| Polyamorous Relationships | | | | | | | |
| Pony/Puppy Training | | | | | | | |
| Riding Crop | | | | | | | |
| Sensory Deprivation | | | | | | | |
| Spanking/Paddling | | | | | | | |
| Tattoos | | | | | | | |
| Tickling | | | | | | | |
| Watersports | | | | | | | |
| Whips | | | | | | | |

# Chapter Eleven

## Confirming Consent

Whatever acronym you choose to represent your BDSM interactions — SSC, RACK, PRICK, CCC (See Chapter 2) — all have one word in common: *consensual.* Consent is required whatever your partner's gender, orientation, or sexuality.

## Defining Consent

One of the biggest issues that can impede true consent — and cause a scene to go bad, a bottom to believe they've been abused, a Top to feel overwhelmed — is whether consent is implicit or explicit.

**Explicit:**
> fully and clearly expressed or demonstrated; leaving nothing merely implied; unequivocal

**Implicit:**
> indicated or suggested, without being directly or explicitly stated; tacitly understood

**Explicit Consent:**
> permission, approval, agreement

**Implicit Consent:**
> compliance or acquiescence

# Obtaining Consent

Whether you define a period of time during which two or more people will engage in sadomasochistic activities and/or exchange some level of power, or you create a total power exchange relationship, you must obtain consent. Even *consensual non-consent* must allow all parties to be able to make an independent decision to walk away.

# Consensual Non-Consent

The collar around my submissive's neck doesn't have a clasp. My initial is branded on his bicep. I make all decisions about how he lives: from the small ones (about food, clothing, and daily activities) to the large ones (about taxes, investments, and property). But, he is not my slave. If one of us ever decided that leaving me was in his or my best interest, he knows I would not throw him out with no resources. Sometimes ceding control to me chafes, but he stays because he loves me and he wants to be with me. That's consensual non-consent.

# Avoiding Abuse

If you ever feel trapped in a situation or relationship, consent has not been defined or obtained.

I've discussed ways to identify abuse masquerading as BDSM. Now, I'd like to discuss how to avoid abuse by *obtaining explicit consent*.

Before you attempt to do any scene — online or in person — it is critical that you and your partner or partners negotiate exactly what that scene will entail.

- How long will it last?
- Will it involve pain and/or bondage?
- Will it include role playing?
- Will you wear costumes?
- Will your clothing get torn?
- What kind of sexual interaction, if any, will be permitted?
- Will you use barriers?
- What fluids, if any, will be exchanged?
- Have you discussed STDs, hepatitis, and other blood-borne diseases?
- How much control is the bottom giving to the Top?
- Will you script out the scene to the last detail or just define your roles and see where that takes you?

# Negotiations

You absolutely *must* complete negotiations before the scene begins. Once you start playing, getting the bottom to agree to anything not originally covered is coercion. Unless you have progressed to the level of *non-consent* (which should never be considered except in long-term, established relationships), the bottom must have a way — and permission — to stop the scene.

During negotiations that define the parameters of your scene, the bottom must freely consent to exactly how much power the Top will have. Especially if this is your or their first scene of this kind, it's better to take the time to go over all the options and thoroughly discuss what's going to take place.

The length and details of negotiations should be inversely proportional to the amount of time a person has been involved in BDSM — the less experience, the more time and details required. However, the time and level of detail spent on negotiations should be inversely proportional to the person who has had the *least* amount of experience. In other words, if you have someone who's been practicing BDSM for a decade negotiating with someone new to the scene, the negotiations need to be structured to accommodate the latter, not the former.

You can't legitimately negotiate or obtain consent from someone who doesn't understand what they're consenting to. Between two experienced practitioners, negotiations may only require a few sentences — and, if they're partners, a few words. But when a beginner is involved, it may take hours or even days and involve lengthy checklists of what the beginner is willing to try, with detailed explanations of what those things are.

# Embarrassing Turn-Ons

Negotiating consent with a beginner must take into account

that many beginners find their own fetishes embarrassing. As mentioned in the Introduction, our society has a lot of hang-ups when it comes to sex. The holy rollers have made it illegal to purchase dildoes and other sex toys in more than one state in the U.S. Adult shops, bookstores, websites, and swingers' clubs have been closed down across the country under various pretexts ranging from outright obscenity charges to prohibitive business licensing requirements. Consensual sadomasochistic activities aren't legal in some jurisdictions. Erotic literature and nonfiction books about sex are hidden from search engines. ISP filters to "protect" children from porn, are more likely to prevent educational material from being available to adults.

So, if someone is horrified that the idea of being tied up turns them on, that needs to be addressed first. Likewise, if someone expresses a willingness to participate in activities just to satisfy their partner or playmate — even though they don't find the idea appealing at all — that needs to be discussed *before* negotiations even start.

It's only too easy for a charismatic Top to convince a vulnerable and perhaps gullible partner to try things totally outside of their comfort zone. One person's wildest, most outrageous sex act is what another person considers plain old vanilla. For some people oral or anal sex is quite adventurous. For others, while either might be enjoyable, those activities are a little tame. It's critical for a more experienced partner to acknowledge how outrageous their activities might seem to someone who has never tried them and/or who was raised to think they are something nasty that only prostitutes engage in.

# Lists and Definitions

In order to avoid the problems caused by a discrepancy in experience or desire, it's sometimes best *not* to conduct negotiations face to face.

As I mentioned, employing checklists with detailed definitions and explanations can often be a good starting point. You can create your own, or find them online. The more-experienced partner should be prepared to answer questions, but the less-experienced partner should also do their own research online or in books. How well the less-experienced partner knows the more-experienced partner needs to be factored into any information exchange.

If you've met someone online you plan to play with and know little about them, they should not be the one answering your questions about fetishes and safety (unless they're giving you links to established websites which verify their information).

It's critical that the person who will be the Top has a list of, and understands, any physical limitations or medical issues the bottom has. Even if the encounter is via computer or phone, the Top needs to know if the bottom can't kneel for long periods or must stop at some point to take medication. Since, online, a Top can't monitor a bottom's temperature, how flushed they are, or whether their circulation has been cut off, verbal status checks need to be more frequent and explicit.

Your play may or may not involve actual sexual intercourse, however you define that. But it's important to determine whether or not and what type of intercourse will be acceptable, as part of *negotiations* and not after play gets you all hot and bothered.

Giving someone power for a scene doesn't mean you've given them any control over your life. Trust me, I'm a FemDom, and although I've bottomed in scene for specific reasons, I never give up control to anyone. Power exchange for the purpose of a *single* encounter is just that — "We're going to do this and then we'll go back to the normal dynamics of our relationship." — whether the relationship is online only or a long-time marriage.

## Respect, Communication, Trust

Erotic power exchange, bondage, and sadomasochism are very personal and intimate activities that can create an intensity you may never have experienced. Therefore, I recommend that you evaluate your relationship vulnerability levels before getting involved.

Three things are critical to the foundation of any relationship, but especially one that includes kinky activities. (For this discussion, relationship ranges from planning play with someone you just met online to years living together and includes everything in between.)

- ✧ The first is respect. Any relationship should be based on mutual respect, but respect is especially critical if you're going to accept or cede control. If you have doubts that you have the respect of your partner or playmate, or that you respect them, it is very likely there is something wrong with the relationship. While erotic power exchange can spice things up, it alone is not going to resolve any fundamental problems.
- ✧ The second is communication. Communication is paramount

and it's a two-way street. If you feel your arguments, feelings, and thoughts are being disregarded, or if you believe your partner/playmate is not sharing with you their feelings and concerns, you have stumbled on a warning signal. You need to resolve those issues before negotiating anything kinky.

⬥ The third foundation is trust. Even if you just met at a party or you've known each other for years, whether you live together or you're halfway across the country (or on the other side of the world) from the person you're involved with, can you trust them to not hurt you?

# When Things Go Wrong

Negotiations also should include a discussion of what will happen if something goes wrong. Sometimes we are better off masturbating to our fantasies rather than acting them out. Once you get started, it's possible for someone to freak, especially if the scene triggers a memory of something in the past that they haven't come to terms with emotionally.

If you're the bottom and you find yourself going someplace you're not sure you can manage emotionally, it's important for you to use your safeword.

But it's also the duty and responsibility of the Top to watch for signs of distress in their partner, especially if they try to push limits. The Top needs to be able to stop the scene, whether they perceive a problem or the bottom uses their safeword.

In either case, the Top then needs to give the bottom comfort to get over whatever caused them emotional or physical distress.

For someone whose repressed traumatic childhood memories have been triggered, that care and comfort may take several days and may even require professional help. (This happens, but it's rare, and I don't want the thought to scare you off. I just want you to understand there is such a risk, because I believe it's better to be prepared for the unlikely possibility than to be caught off guard.)

## Aftercare

Even when a scene goes well, you will still want to have negotiated time for aftercare. This is usually something the Top gives to the bottom to help them ease out of subspace back into the real world. But often Tops need aftercare as well. If you just literally or figuratively pissed all over your partner (even if they loved it) you may have to come to terms with the fact that it turned you on. You may need reassurance that the bottom really enjoyed the scene, and that they appreciate your willingness to push your own limits to please them.

Both Top and bottom, may have gone into a completely different head space during the scene, and they need some time to decompress. "Wham, bam, thank you ma'am" is not an appropriate ending to this kind of interaction. Before the scene, discuss how much time you'll want to allow afterwards to talk and take care of each other. Make sure you address hydration and nutritional needs, especially after a lengthy and/or intense scene.

## Processing Your Reactions

If you're new, or this is the first time you've played with someone, you probably want to process the scene separately, first. Then, a day or two after, you can discuss it together. You should think about what you liked, what you didn't like, how you felt, what did or didn't meet your expectations. Then sit down with your partner and discuss these things.

The conclusions from that conversation should guide you in future scenes. You'll want to figure out how to duplicate what went right (without repeating the same thing over and over again, of course) and how to avoid what went wrong. And wrong and right are defined strictly by what you both did and didn't enjoy in the scene.

# Chapter Twelve
# Courting a FemDom

## Disadvantages

If you identify as a male submissive or male bottom and you want to find a FemDom online, you have a number of disadvantages.

First, you're competing for each FemDom's attention with dozens, or even hundreds of other males (depending on her age and attractiveness).

Second, you're faced with a dichotomy between your desire and hers. You want a woman who will take charge. She still expects to be courted. You desire someone who will make all the decisions, including finding you online, figuring out what you need from the three words you put on your profile, and forcefully fulfilling your fantasies. She's looking for someone to take her out to dinner, detail her car, pick up her dry cleaning, and scrub her toilets.

On the other hand, it's not difficult to stand out from the crowd, when the crowd behaves in ways most FemdDoms find unappealing.

## Dos and Don'ts

So, how do you court a FemDom online? First and foremost, recognize that FemDoms are people. We're all individuals with different desires, kinks, and wishes.

### DON'T

- Ask a FemDom a question she already made a point of answering in her profile.
- Ignore her specific instructions on how she wishes to be approached.
- Send her the same message you sent every other FemDom who meets your search parameters, especially one-line, meaningless platitudes.
- Use crude language or talk about sex before she's opened that topic of conversation.
- Send her a picture of your cock (unless she's asked for one).
- Send a "friend" request before exchanging any correspondence.
- Contact someone who says she's not interested in online if you're only able/willing to do online.

- ✧ Hold yourself out as someone interested in service when you're only looking for a play partner.
- ✧ Assume that just because she's a FemDom she will be interested in certain things.
- ✧ Ask her to "train" you.
- ✧ Tell her you'll do anything she wants, then refuse her first request.
- ✧ Stalk her by sending her message after unanswered message, finding her on other social media sites, or creating another profile (because she's blocked the one you initially used to contact her).
- ✧ Follow her around like a puppy at parties unless that's her kink and she's invited you to do so.
- ✧ Refuse to accept no for an answer.
- ✧ Call her Mistress unless she's instructed you to do so.
- ✧ Call her a Dominatrix or offer to buy her time.

## DO

- ✧ Read her profile carefully and answer any questions she asks in your first email.
- ✧ Write specifics about why her particular profile appeals to you. (Hint, it's not because she's a FemDom or because you like her photograph.)
- ✧ Let her know what you can offer her based on *her* profile, not on what you believe all FemDoms want.
- ✧ Be polite and respectful without being ingratiating.
- ✧ Proofread your email. (You don't want anyone to misinterpret

what you've said because you used the wrong word or punctuation.)
- Let her know what skills you have, classes you've taken, or books you've read that will help you meet the needs she's specified.
- Treat her like a person first and a FemDom second.
- After you've corresponded, if her responses have been positive, then ask her out for a drink or coffee or lunch. Let her choose how much of a commitment she's willing to make. If she's agreed to a drink don't try to badger her into dinner.
- Pick up the check.

# Chapter Thirteen

## A Word On ProDommes (aka Dominatrixes)

ProDommes (aka Dominatrixes) have a unique place among sex professionals. At least in the United States, mostPro-Dommes don't have any form of sexual contact with their clients, and yet they're considered sex workers. In some states, even though they do not permit genital contact, their activities are still illegal.

For the record, I do not believe sex work should be illegal. I respect those who choose to do it as long as they are honest in presenting themselves as such.

Visiting a ProDomme can be expensive, especially if they're

young and pretty. Sessions can range from several hundred dollars an hour on up.

But, bear in mind that working as a ProDomme is incredibly costly. They must purchase elegant clothing, high-priced tools and furniture, and procure appropriate space.

The advantage of purchasing an expensive session from a ProDomme is that they deliver precisely what their clients request (within their own specified restrictions). They will wear the stereotypical clothing and use the client's preferred language.

Given the limited options available on most fetish sites, men who identify as "submissive" often do not realize they are actually bottoms. Male submissives, men who want or choose to serve a woman exactly how that woman prefers, are rarer than male bottoms.

While many FemDoms enjoy playing with bottoms, most are looking for more than just someone who wants her to beat their ass. They want a relationship, just one structured differently than what is considered the norm.

So, if you're a bottom looking for a specific experience, especially if you don't have the time to court a FemDom or are already in a relationship, visiting a ProDomme may be your best option if you can afford it.

ProDommes offer the *illusion* of dominance while still delivering exactly the type of interaction desired. Few ProDommes are also FemDoms. (When a client gives you money to do what they want, the client with the money is the one in control.)

Note, those ProDommes who are FemDoms typically keep

their clients separate from their personal life. Just because she has accepted you as a client does not mean she would consider you as her own personal submissive/slave.

# Chapter Fourteen

## Munches

### What is a Munch?

If you decide you want to venture out into public to explore kink in real life, the most logical place to start is your local munch. A munch is a regular gathering of folks interested in and/or participating in kink. Most munches meet at a vanilla location such as a coffee shop, restaurant, or bar. Even smaller towns can have a monthly munch if enough folks are interested. In bigger cities, you're likely to find a variety of munches: they cater to folks with different schedules, meet as often as weekly, and some are open only to specific genders, orientations, interests, or ages.

Munches range in size from a designated table in a corner for a few kinksters to a private room filled with dozens of people. Most munches depend on the goodwill of the venue for providing them the space to meet. That means people are expected to purchase a beverage or food to support that venue. It also means that folks who attend the munch should avoid doing anything that will alienate the venue's other customers.

# Attending a Munch

When you arrive, no one may acknowledge you or there may be a host who will greet you and introduce you around on your first visit. Some munches even have name tags (you use only a first name or a scene name). Munches are often very unstructured. People come and go within the allotted time frame, and not everyone will stay for the entire event. You might hear announcements from local organizations or find fliers on the table for area events. Other munches have demos, speakers, programs, and/or vendor displays.

Mostly, munches are a place for those curious about kink to meet others who are involved in it. Fetish attire is worn only by those who are completely out about their BDSM involvement (and then only if it's appropriate for the venue). Unless the room is very private, you're not likely to see S&M play, and any Master/slave interactions will be very covert.

You may find it difficult to determine who's a Dominant and who's a submissive at a munch. Whatever someone's orientation, your interaction with them should be polite and respectful. Just because someone identifies as a submissive, doesn't mean they're in service to anyone but their own Dominant. Just because someone identifies as a Dominant doesn't mean they expect (or want) anyone but their own submissive in service to them.

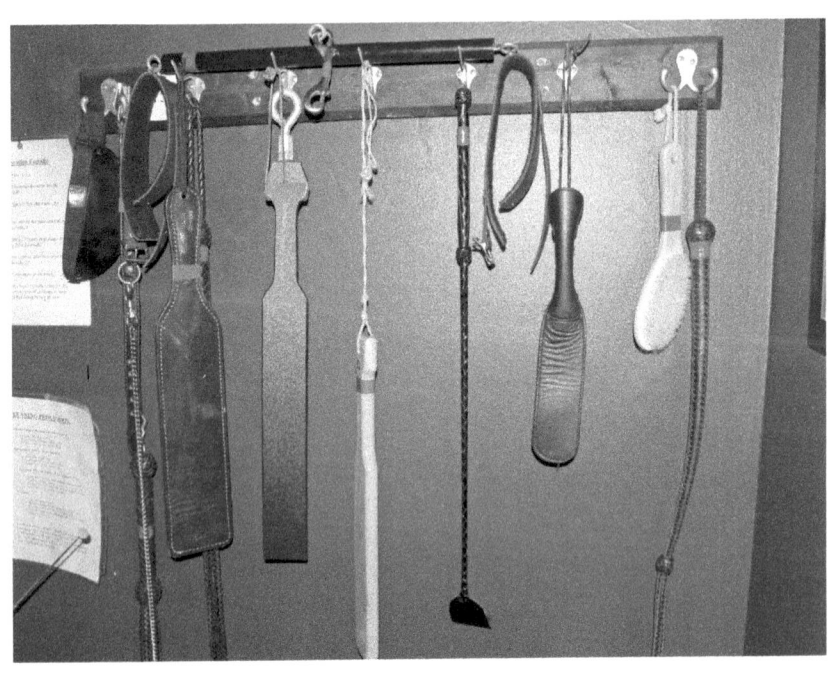

# Chapter Fifteen
## What About Dungeons?

### Finding a Dungeon

If you live in a large enough metropolitan area, there may be semi-public play spaces accessible for the price of membership. You may be required to sit through some sort of initiation/introduction, which is a great way to get an idea of what is and what isn't permitted.

In mid-size cities, there might be an organization that holds play parties on a regular or semi-regular basis. Usually you will find out about those via the local munch or by joining the organization that hosts the parties.

In many communities, semi-private dungeons are operated by

individuals — some to subsidize the play spaces they build for themselves, some to just share their space with friends.

In those cases especially, the owners will want to get to know you before they invite you into what most likely is their private home. You're liable to meet them at a munch, a class, or a workshop. They need to believe they can trust you not to reveal their home address, that none of their other guests have anything to fear from you, and that you won't out them to someone, accidentally or on purpose.

Dungeons can range in size from a room in someone's basement to an entire commercial building. They might have two or three pieces of equipment or dozens. The equipment may be permanently installed or brought in and set up for specific occasions and then stored the rest of the time in someone's house or a locker.

## Dungeon Etiquette

Dungeon rules vary as much as size and equipment options. Most dungeons will post their rules or provide them to you in the form of a handout. You have an obligation to learn the rules for the dungeon you visit and to follow them. You may have to sign a release form. Chances are that unless you are attending a private party in a private play space, you will be required to produce legal identification.

Find out what is expected in terms of apparel before you show up in street clothes only to learn that fetish attire is required. Don't strip down to your birthday suit until you learn if that's acceptable.

Expect to be required to put your cell phone away (and preferably off) for the evening. Cameras on mobile phones have become ubiquitous, and people don't want to be photographed in a dungeon. Then too, no one wants their subspace or topspace interrupted by an obnoxious ringtone.

In all dungeons, respect is required. Don't touch anything or anyone without permission. Don't get in the way of a player's back swing — they're focused on their partner, so they can't pay attention to someone who walks too close behind them.

Many public players are exhibitionists, and they enjoy being watched, but not if the spectators get in the way of their whips or their head space.

Don't crowd a scene or try to chat with the participants. Players seek a mental state that you interrupt when you gawk, stand too close, masturbate, or talk in anything louder than a whisper.

If you see something interesting and want to ask questions, wait until the scene is over and the players have moved to the social area. Many times folks are willing to share their experience and expertise, but not while they're playing or giving/receiving aftercare.

If you see something you believe to be dangerous, do not interrupt the scene. Speak to a dungeon monitor or the party host. Almost certainly if the players are engaged in a heavy or edgy scene, they have let the people responsible for the party know.

If you see kink that squicks or freaks you out, move out of sight of the scene. We all have our own comfort zone. That zone will usually enlarge as you gain more experience. But, unless you're the dungeon monitor and the players are violating party/dungeon rules, you have *no* business interfering with someone else's play.

If you see someone you think you'd like to play with, ask them if they're interested when they're *not* playing. Don't be surprised, disappointed, or childish if they say no. Some people only play with their long-time partners. Some only play with people they know well. Others are open to playing with someone they just met at a party. You won't know until you ask. Just be respectful and polite and be willing to accept a negative answer graciously.

If you want to play with someone who wears a collar, find out if you should ask that person or the person who owns them, first.

# Chapter Sixteen

## Resources

The Internet is not a stable place. Any links I put here would have to be typed in by those who purchased the print book, and they might change the day after the book is published. Plus I find new links and books all the time that would be missing from here.

So, I have created, and will maintain, a resource page on my website. You can find it by scrolling down to the bottom bar on any page, or by going directly to:

www.eroticawriter.net/resources.php

And, if you live in a repressive country such as the U.K. (or, for that matter, the U.S.) and have difficulty accessing my site, you can find the same information at:

http://frederickbooks.com/resources.php

**Have Fun. Stay Safe.**

# Fiction from Pussy Cat Press
## By I.G. Frederick includes:
# Complicated Couplings
### Four sexy stories about tangled twosomes

*"If You Love Someone"* — Tara leaves her husband to move in with Nathan, but he abandons her after a few months. When he returns, begging her to take him back, life and love look very different.

*"Commiserate"* — The same man dumped them both. When they commiserate, they discover more in common than an ex-boyfriend.

*"Passion's Price"* — Richard steals Gina's heart from three thousand miles away. But, when he moves across the country, her intensity and passion for life drive him away.

*"Lunchtime Lover"* — Both married, they started their affair with the promise never to fall in love. Then Lisa's divorce becomes final.

www.eroticawriter.net/ComplicatedCouplings.html

# Cougar Conquests

## Beautiful older women on the prowl and the sweet young cubs captured by their allure

*"Benjamin"* — *A chance meeting at a munch in a tiny town leads Benjamin to an opportunity for training. But, Lady Gina tries to end the relationship rather than emotionally torture herself.*

*"Festival of Eros"* — *The handsome young man followed her around all evening, behaving like the perfect submissive … until she learned his identity.*

*"Paddles"* — *A biker bar with no bikers? The decor, name, and patrons of a bar in a small Eastern Oregon town puzzle William who just stopped in for a beer. Then the owner introduces him to the secrets of this very special tavern.*

*"Starting Over"* — *When her pet walked out on her, she stayed away from parties because it hurt to watch other women playing with their toys. But, a friend coerces her into attending a unique event.*

*"The Cougar and the College Boys"* — *Alone in the woods, hours from Portland, Tess discovers four college friends staying in a nearby cabin. The boys invite her to share their campfire, their dinner, and …*

www.eroticawriter.net/CougarConquests.html

# Dommemoir

# WARNING:
## This book changes women's attitudes about relationship dynamics, forever.

*In Geneviéve's journey of discovery she dabbles in the BDSM lifestyle, which forces her to recognize and acknowledge her true nature. Her memoir, woven together with that of a male slave, draws the reader into an intense odyssey of sexual expression triumphing over sexual repression while delivering fascinating insight into a different kind of love.*

*"The aptly titled* Dommemoir *delivers on so many levels... It quickly sucks you in and envelops you in the bondage of its spell...* Dommemoir *is a character study that breathes complex and compelling life into its hero, the devastating Lady Geneviéve, and the fortunate submissives who worship at her feet... placing you in the delicious bondage of its dark and compelling landscape..."*

                      **Larry Brooks, USA Today bestselling author of**
                              *Darkness Bound* **and** *Bait and Switch*

## www.eroticawriter.net/Dommemoir.html

# Eleanor & Mick

## A journey of sexual exploration and insight

*In five sizzling hot stories, Eleanor seeks refuge in a small town on the Oregon Coast and befriends her younger neighbor. He captures first her heart and then her submission, taking her on a journey of sexual exploration and insight.*

*"Salt for His Wounds" — When Eleanor's ex-husband shows up begging for a second chance, she asks her young, gorgeous next door neighbor for a favor and Mick takes advantage of the opportunity.*

*"The Mercantile" — Eleanor attributes Mick's detachment to the difference in their ages, but Mick confesses a need for kink. Afraid of losing him, Eleanor reluctantly consents to bondage and pain.*

*"The Things We Do for Love" — When her gorgeous girlfriend visits Eleanor on the coast, Mick's obvious attraction troubles her. But, Liz only has eyes for Eleanor.*

*"Paid in Full" — Mick's army buddy finds Eleanor hot and makes a deal with Mick. But, if Mick really loved Eleanor would he let another man have sex with her?*

*"Renovations" — After Mick spends a month renovating their garage, Eleanor discovers he built in a few surprises.*

# www.eroticawriter.net/EleanorMick.html

# Family Dynamics

## Six sultry stories exploring sexuality in Dominant/submissive liaisons

*"'Aunt' Grace"* — Jen needed a place to stay in Portland and turned to her father's stepsister. But, she found so much more than she ever dreamed possible with her "Aunt" Grace. Second Place, NLA:I John Preston Short Story Award.

*"Leather Family"* — Kyle needs his own boy. Jacques would do almost anything to find a place in a Leather Family. But, Kyle serves a female Master.

*"Searching"* — Two Dominants love each other but need someone who submits to them both. Just how far will young Jeremy go to serve the lovely Lady Theresa?

*"Taking Control"* — To free the woman she loves from a horrid sadist's perverted games, Melanie must set aside her own aversion to men.

*"Family Ties"* — When her slave's ex faces eviction, Katherine offers refuge. But can Naomi pay the price?

*"Said the Unicorn"* — Tessa dedicates herself to her Master's service, so his determination to add another woman to their family devastates her.

## www.eroticawriter.net/FamilyDynamics.html

# Fork In The Road

**Changing people's lives and relationships in three pairs of sexy stories**

*"Said the Unicorn" — Tessa dedicates herself to her Master's service, so his determination to add another woman to their family devastates her.*

*"Proposals" — The evening appears perfectly arranged for him to pop the question. But, Christopher's proposition takes Geraldine on an unanticipated sexual adventure.*

*"Winners & Losers" — When he finally walks away from the blackjack table, Jeffrey finds someone worth gambling on.*

www.eroticawriter.net/ForkinRoad.html

# Ladies in Love

**Six sizzling stories of Lesbian Lust**

*"Empty Seat" — Laura offers Alex a nightcap as thanks for her help with a presentation to a prospective client. But they never order drinks.*

*"'Aunt' Grace" — Jen needed a place to stay in Portland and turned to her father's stepsister. But, she found so much more than she ever dreamed possible with her "Aunt" Grace. Second Place, NLA:I John Preston Short Story Award.*

*"Spa Date" — Dismayed that she introduced Sam to the woman who betrayed her, Julie tries to play matchmaker again.*

*"Taking Control"* — To free the woman she loves from a horrid sadist's perverted games, Melanie must set aside her own aversion to men.

*"Dental School"* — How can Cindy flirt with the beautiful blonde dental instructor while her mother tries to fix Cindy up with the male student examining her teeth?

*"Commiserate"* — The same man dumped them both. When they commiserate, they discover more in common than an ex-boyfriend.

www.eroticawriter.net/LadiesinLove.html

# Leather Home

**Sometimes love takes us to strange places before it brings us home.**

*"Theresa"* — Richard admits to boorish behavior, but Theresa has no use for his apology. Then, he persuades her to accept a ride home from him and proves his integrity.

*"Richard"* — Lady Theresa fascinated Richard from the first time he saw her. But, how does he convince her to consider a more than casual relationship with a dominant male?

*"Searching"* — Two Dominants love each other but need someone who submits to them both. Just how far will young Jesse go to serve the lovely Lady Theresa?

*"Jesse"* — Jesse finds the perfect Mistress, the woman he trained all his life to serve. Unfortunately, her husband also finds Jesse attractive.

http://www.eroticawriter.net/LeatherHome.html

# Lessons Learned

## Sometimes you need more than love

*Four sizzling hot FemDom love stories about women who come to terms with their dominant sides and discover that this makes them more attractive to the men they love.*

*"Tea Party" — What if the first time your best friend drags you to a FemDom "Tea Party" you see your former boyfriend serving canapes naked?*

*"Blind Date" — How do you respond when you find your ex-husband hanging out at the restaurant where you planned to meet your "Blind Date"?*

*"To Serve" — If you love a vanilla woman and you only want "To Serve," how do you introduce her to the lifestyle without scaring her away?*

*"Change in View" — What if a "Change in View" alters the attitude of the man you mentored so he could find his perfect Mistress?*

www.eroticawriter.net/LessonsLearned.html

# Love Hurts

## but in a good way

### Five steamy stories about the dark side of love

*"B&D Trainee"* —Online, Xavier promised to make his B&D fantasies come true. But, had he jumped in over his head?

*"Knife Play"* — Seeking a knife he saw online, Jack inadvertently found himself in a room full of pain and bondage contraptions. He almost turned around and left, but a beautiful woman taught him a different way to appreciate blades.

*"Pussy Whipped"* — Eric knew nothing about BDSM, but purchased a ticket to a fundraiser to help out his friends. When Miranda asks him to "play," he discovers exactly what those four letters mean.

*"The Auction"* —He attended the auction with only one goal: to acquire a very special whip. But an offer to try it out proved irresistible and he discovered that sometimes events, and women, can exceed one's expectations.

*"FemDom Fairy Tale"* — A FemDom's offhand remark about a photograph at an erotic art show draws a handsome man's attention. But, when two Dominants find each other attractive, which one chooses to kneel? (First published in Desire Presents.)

www.eroticawriter.net/LoveHurts.html

# Second Chances

## Six sexy stories about getting a second shot at the gold ring

*"Back to School"* — *An admin error forces Jordan and Dennis to share a dorm room. Older than their classmates, they decide to stick together. But Jordan's past threatens to keep them apart.*

*"Gordon"* — *When the cover model of her latest book walks into the coffee shop where she writes, Lenore embarrassingly calls him by her character's name. His reaction confounds her.*

*"Spa Date"* — *Dismayed that she introduced Sam to the woman who betrayed her, Julie tries to play matchmaker again.*

*"Salt for His Wounds"* — *When Eleanor's ex-husband shows up begging for a second chance, she asks her young, gorgeous next door neighbor for a favor. Mick takes advantage of the opportunity.*

*"Proposal: Tangled Webs"* — *The evening appears perfectly arranged for him to pop the question. But, Christopher's proposition takes Geraldine on an unanticipated sexual adventure.*

*"Starting Over"* — *When her pet walked out on her, she stayed away from parties because it hurt to watch other women playing with their toys. But, a friend coerces her into attending a unique event.*

# www.eroticawriter.net/SecondChances.html

# When Two's Not Enough
## Seven sexy ménage stories

*"Tribal Fusion"* — Wherever he dances, Dominic collects propositions, but the Lady Lenore's proposal takes him by surprise.

*"Two Brothers"* — A divorcée in a flashy sports car attracts the attention of two young virgin brothers visiting the "big" city of Boise.

*"Honeymoon"* — Although she expected to honeymoon aboard a cruise ship, Allison finds herself sailing on a private yacht staffed by an incredibly beautiful couple. Convinced her new husband wants to hide his older, less attractive wife, she finds it difficult to enjoy the hedonistic delights offered in paradise.

*"Jail Bait"* — Serena wants Joshua to pop her cherry, but he won't touch her because of her age. When her birthday finally makes it legal, he arranges for a very special celebration.

*"Nikki's Birthday"* — Even someone happy in a monogamous relationship might find the gift of a hot, new toy for an evening of decadence incredibly exciting.

*"Market Boy"* — When a beautiful Domme offers Jack the opportunity to serve at a party for her friends, he responds too quickly and too eagerly, getting more than he bargained for.

*"The Cougar and the College Boys"* — Alone in the woods, hours from Portland, Tess discovers four college friends staying in a nearby cabin. The boys invite her to share their campfire, their dinner, and …

## www.eroticawriter.net/TwoNotEnough.html

# Who Tops Who?
## when dynamic Dominants find each other irresistible

*"Chocolate Cake" — Her submissive toys wait for her at home, but Louise finds an offer by an attractive Dom as tempting as Chocolate Cake. (First published in One Night Only: Explicit Erotica, edited by Violet Blue.)*

*"FemDom Fairy Tale" — A FemDom's offhand remark about a photograph at an erotic art show draws a handsome man's attention. But, when two Dominants find each other attractive, which one chooses to kneel? (First published in Desire Presents.)*

*"Switch" — Liza found it difficult to maintain control around Emanuel, but she found his offer to share his slave with her irresistible.*

*"Theresa" — Richard admits to boorish behavior, but Theresa has no use for his apology. Then, he persuades her to accept a ride home from him and proves his integrity.*

http://www.eroticawriter.net/WhoTopsWho.html

# Young & Eager
## Barely legal but hardly innocent

*"Two Brothers" — A divorcée in a flashy sports car attracts the attention of two young virgin brothers visiting the "big" city of Boise.*

*"Teachers Pet" — Trapped at an all-girls' school in the middle of nowhere, Sabrina tries to get her hunky teacher to bust her cherry.*

"Arresting Development" — Bethany went out with Officer Rick to avoid a speeding ticket, but discovered she enjoyed getting "arrested."

"Jail Bait" — Serena wants Joshua to pop her cherry, but he won't touch her because of her age. When her birthday finally makes it legal, he arranges for a very special celebration.

www.eroticawriter.net/YoungEager.html

visit
http://eroticawriter.net/
to find links to individual stories
and additional collections
and

**For darker, edgier fiction**
# NOVELS BY
# KORIN I. DUSHAYL

## The Darker Side of Intimacy

# PLAYING WITH DOLLS

## "a must read for anyone who ever had to learn how to be comfortable in their own skin"

*Jesse enjoys playing with dolls and wearing girls' clothing and everyone from his parents, teachers, friends and neighbors assumes he will grow up gay. As an adult the burden of those assumptions hampers his ability to come to terms with his sexuality"*

*Korin I. Dushayl "has accomplished something remarkable here, crafting a story that works on all levels — educating, arousing, inspiring, empowering, and (most importantly) emotionally connecting with the reader."*

*Sally Bibrary, Bending the Bookshelf*

**http://transgressivewriter.com/dolls.php**

# BROKEN

## Some things can never be fixed

*Given a choice between slavery and ostracization, Jessica chooses to kneel naked before her department head so she can continue studying for her PhD in psychology. That decision takes her down a dark path to abuse, exploitation, and torment of both her body and her spirit.*

*Korin I. Dushayl "writes with authority and compassion about those who live within the lifestyle. Broken and Shattered explore issues including finding and initiating a submissive partner, informed consent, and the difference between dominating someone and exploiting their needs."*

*Elizabeth Coldwell*
*author, anthologist, magazine editor*

http://transgressivewriter.com/broken.php

# SHATTERED

**Just where do you cross the point of no return?**

*When a sweet, intelligent twenty-five year old with undiagnosed Asperser and PTSD seeks help from a ruthless, unscrupulous, sadistic therapist, she shatters his psyche and throws him into a suicidal depression. Her crude attempt to pick up the pieces -- enslaving him and subjecting him to unethical, unsanctioned, experiments -- ignores the lines of consent and the responsibilities of a Dominant. -- Inspired by a true story.*

*"The work ... unfolds with the assured touch of a bestselling mainstream author, seducing us into the lives of people with needs and agendas that find wings in the dark. Only an author familiar with this landscape could peel back these layers of psychological complexity without flinching and without dramatic compromise*

*... Prepare to submit to this reading experience, which will mark you with its narrative power.*

*Larry Brooks, USA Today bestselling author of Darkness Bound and Bait and Switch*

http://transgressivewriter.com/shattered.php

# CHOICES

*Must Linda's sexual awakening destroy her marriage?*

*From fairy tales to modern legal tradition, society demands we love exclusively, even though many only find happiness with multiple partners. Linda finally confronts long neglected sexual needs when Phil forces himself on her in Chicago. But back in Portland, her husband's insistence on monogamy compels her to choose between his limitations and her own insatiable desires.*

http://transgressivewriter.com/choices.php

# THE LADY & THE SPYDER

## A BDSM Space Opera

*Centuries ago, theocratic governments subjugated the last resistance on Earth. Those unwilling to tolerate the religious bigotry, fled the planet seeking a new beginning among the stars.*

*Generations later, their descendants found a new home in a far away system.*

*But no matter how far humans travel, greed and the desire for control journey with them and now the specter of intolerance rises again.*

*The Lady Cassandra -- FemDom, slave owner, Dominatrix -- finds her lifestyle and her livelihood threatened by a fast-rising fanatical movement founded by a former client. Her alpha slave, Captain Varyl Malonds aka Spyder -- smuggler and superb pilot with incredible tactical skills -- risks his ship, his income, and even his life for his Lady.*

http://transgressivewriter.com/spyder.php

## visit
## transgressivewriter.com

www.ingramcontent.com/pod-product-compliance
Lightning Source LLC
Chambersburg PA
CBHW061444040426
42450CB00007B/1202